THINK *Like* GOD

*To Ann Clones
Blessing*

RICHARD C. GAYLE

THINK LIKE GOD
Copyright © 2018 by Richard C. Gayle

All rights reserved. Neither this publication nor any part of this publication may be reproduced or transmitted in any form or by any means, electronic or mechanical, including photocopying, recording or any information storage and retrieval system, without permission in writing from the author.

The views and opinions expressed in this publication belong solely to the author, and do not reflect those of Word Alive Press or any of its employees.

Unless otherwise indicated, all scripture quotations taken from the Holy Bible, King James Version, which is in the public domain. Scripture quotations marked (NKJV) taken from the New King James Version®. Copyright © 1982 by Thomas Nelson. Used by permission. All rights reserved. Scripture quotations marked (NIV) are taken from the Holy Bible, New International Version®, NIV®. Copyright © 1973, 1978, 1984, 2011 by Biblica, Inc.™ Used by permission of Zondervan. All rights reserved worldwide. www.zondervan.com The "NIV" and "New International Version" are trademarks registered in the United States Patent and Trademark Office by Biblica, Inc.™ Scripture quotations taken from the New American Standard Bible® (NASB), Copyright © 1960, 1962, 1963, 1968, 1971, 1972, 1973, 1975, 1977, 1995 by The Lockman Foundation. Used by permission. www.Lockman.org

Printed in Canada

ISBN: 978-1-4866-1630-5

Word Alive Press
119 De Baets Street, Winnipeg, MB R2J 3R9
www.wordalivepress.ca

Cataloguing in Publication may be obtained through Library and Archives Canada

To my mother, Auntie Mommy, who has always kept me before the Lord in her prayers; my boys, Richard and Michael, who have been the joy of my life since their birth; and my church family, which has helped me grow and develop into the pastor I am. I truly have a great support team, and without their help and dedication this book would not be possible.

Above all, to my God, who has chosen to reveal Himself to me and placed me on this journey—to Him be all the praise and glory.

Contents

	Preface	vii
1.	The Possibilities of the Mind	1
2.	Capturing the Thoughts of God	5
3.	How Does God Think?	11
4.	Examining Our Limitations	16
5.	Restoring the Order	24
6.	Two Worlds	33
7.	Transforming the Mind	40
8.	Transition into the Kingdom of God	46
9.	Think Like God	61

Preface

I am passionate about sharing this book with you, not only because my relationship with God has drastically changed my life, but because I believe it can change yours, too. I've been a Christian for the better part of my life, and in those years I have experienced and witnessed great exploits of God.

However, somewhere along my journey, I began to feel frustrated and confused. If my God is full of possibilities and He can do all things, why does my life not reflect this great God? If He spoke into existence the planet on which we live, why do I feel as if I'm living beneath my God-given privileges and potential? If I'm called to be like Him, why am I so limited? How can I get over those limitations? I understand my finite nature, but I struggle to understand it when I think of the infinite God who lives inside me.

In my quest for answers, this book was birthed. I discovered that God's purpose for sending Jesus Christ to die for our sins was to bring us back to an unhindered relationship with Him by removing the limitations in our minds. Now that we're born again and forgiven of the very sin that separated us from God, we can be more like Him. I realized that to be like Him we must change our human ways of thinking and develop our minds to think like God. When we start doing this, we will be a force to reckon with in this world. I want the world to know God through us. I want us to be the ones the world comes to when they need to find the mind of God.

I pray that the principles of this book will dramatically change your life as they have mine. I pray that you will no longer think like man but instead *think like God*.

chapter one

THE POSSIBILITIES OF THE MIND

THE MIND OF MAN IS AN ENIGMA AND REMAINS A PART OF GOD'S MOST intriguing and fascinating creation. The Psalmist penned it this way: *"I am fearfully and wonderfully made"* (Psalm 139:14).

Of all the wonderful functions of the human body, such as its ability to reproduce and repair itself, the human mind is most mesmerizing. It is what separates us from the animal kingdom. Although we can teach our pets to do great tricks that make us smile, and although we have seen wild animals outsmart our attempts to keep them out of our homes and garbage, none of that compares to what God did with the mind of man! Its ability to make informed decisions and invent incredible machines is unexplainable. It is vast and full of great possibilities. I'm not sure we will ever come to know its full capability.

It is recorded in the book of Daniel that, in the future, *"many shall run to and fro, and knowledge shall be increased"* (Daniel 12:4). Living in this technological age is proof of that. Every day we hear of new innovative ideas and inventions. Everything around us is constantly being improved and changed. A laptop purchased today is replaced tomorrow with a more efficient one. Yesterday's cellphone is no longer sufficient. Medical breakthroughs have caused diseases that once plagued mankind to no longer be problematic.

It's hard sometimes to keep up with all the changes. All these great wonders and advances have come from the mind of man. If we can use our confidence in man's ability to put an airplane in the sky, it should be nothing for us to trust and believe in the One who created that man.

The increase of knowledge, however, doesn't seem to have improved man's relationship with his God. As a matter of fact, it seems to be creating distance between God and man. Man may be thinking that if he can do all these things by himself, he doesn't need God. If a doctor can restore the eyes of the blind, or cause a man to walk again, who needs a miracle?

However, man must realize where his wisdom and knowledge comes from. Proverbs 2:6 tells us that it is the Lord who gives wisdom, and from His mouth come knowledge and understanding. It is clear then that God is the source of wisdom and knowledge. God didn't impart all this wisdom so we can establish a distance from Him, but rather for the wellness and provision of mankind's diverse needs. God wouldn't give us something that would be used against Him.

Romans 1:30 states that there will be *"backbiters, haters of God, despiteful, proud, boasters, inventors of evil things…"* It is obvious that men have used this blessed gift that God gave for his betterment and in turn chose to invent things to bring about his own destruction. Nuclear warheads, fighter jets, and guns are all examples of the destructive use of our great minds. We are exposed to news reports of predators who use great inventions, created for the benefit of society, to lure, manipulate, and rob the unsuspecting. The mind of man can be a dangerous or beautiful thing.

We must not forget, however, that man, as powerful as his mind may be and as great and cunning as he is, is finite. He has boundaries and limits. Man will only be able to go as far as God allows him to go in his research. In Genesis 9, all the men of the earth had one language and one intent, which was to build a tower to reach the heavens. When God saw their oneness of mind, He confounded their language to prevent them from accomplishing this task.

God will never entrust man with certain capabilities which are reserved for the children of the Kingdom. Jesus told the disciples in Matthew 13:11, *"Because it is given unto you to know the mysteries of the kingdom of heaven, but to them it is not given."* There are some things known to people of the Kingdom that the world's greatest scientists do not know. There are some things Kingdom people can do that the greatest archaeologist cannot. Why? Because that wisdom wasn't given to the world; it was given unto us. It was given to us who seek the mind of God.

Can you imagine how great men would become if those with the wisdom of the world, who do not know God, were able to access the thoughts of God in addition to what they already know? I am afraid to think of what

The Possibilities of the Mind

they could do. Better yet, what if we would adapt the tenacity and attitude of the scientist, who spends years in a lab researching, to look deeper into the mysteries of God? I believe we would amaze the world. We wouldn't only be using things already created to make new discoveries; we would be tapping into the mind of God and accessing the unseen world.

In the mind of God lies all the answers scientists have spent their lives searching for. No matter how intelligent a human is, no one is wiser than God. We read in I Corinthians 1:25 that *"the foolishness of God is wiser than men; and the weakness of God is stronger than men."* Not only will we have access to the "foolishness of God," but we will be able to move into the supernatural world. Imagine making it a habit to travel to the supernatural world every morning. It would be nothing for us to be able to call *"those things which be not as though they were"* (Romans 4:17).

If a mind with boundaries and limitations can perform such great exploits, I wonder what would happen if we were to take those limits off the mind of man. Is this possible? Paul said to the Corinthians, *"For who hath known the mind of the Lord, that he may instruct him? But we have the mind of Christ"* (I Corinthians 2:16).

This scripture makes it clear—we have the mind of Christ! But we must tap into it. If we buy a brand new car and park it in our driveway, looking at it every day and commenting on how nice it is and the great places it can take us but never step inside the car, it will never take us anywhere. Unless we allow God to get inside us and let His thoughts rule us, we will never know the greatness that lies within. We must believe that God wants us to expand our minds and capture His thoughts. He wants us to think like Him.

Yes, brothers and sisters, the Bible says we have the mind of Christ.

As I mentioned, if we could put on the attitude of a scientist and spend time daily studying the mind of God through His Word, I believe we would discover some truly amazing and powerful things. Access to this way of thinking is given to us through God's Word. If we diligently read, study, and apply the Word of God, we will see our minds transform into something that reflects the God we worship.

Wow! The finiteness of the mind would be something of the past. This may sound impossible, but with a clear focus and direction, we could train our minds over time. Just like the scientist who pushes and pushes until a cure is found, we will find what we're looking for.

Remember: God cannot trust such knowledge with everyone. That's why He told His disciples that it's not for unbelievers, but rather for us to know the mysteries of the Kingdom. Notice that He didn't refer to the *mystery* of the kingdom, but the *mysteries* of the kingdom. There are many more things about this Kingdom that need to be discovered.

Get ready to be amazed, for we're about to tap into a mind that has no boundaries or limitations—the mind of God.

chapter two
CAPTURING THE THOUGHTS OF GOD

I BELIEVE IT IS POSSIBLE TO CAPTURE THE THOUGHTS OF GOD. TO DO SO, WE MUST be ready to be driven out of our minds, because the thoughts of God are certainly going to blow our minds and disrupt our human ways of thinking.

Remember, God said that His thoughts are higher than the heavens. In capturing the thoughts of God, we must be ready to deal with a higher way of thinking, a way of thinking that will transport us into another world and teach us to think outside our physical laws. Our five senses place limits on our cognitive capacity when we try to obtain God's thoughts (Isaiah 55:8).

We are dealing with a limitless God, a God that is not a man. He said, "I do not think like man. I do not act like man." There is obviously a God-way of thinking and a God-way of doing things. The challenge then is for us to learn how to capture the God-way of thinking while we're still confined to our own way of thinking.

There is always going to be a battle between my way of thinking and the God-way of thinking. How do I overcome this when my human thoughts are still necessary while I'm here in the earthly realm? The primary question then becomes, when do I need to initiate the God-way of thinking? Can I switch from my mind to His?

As humans, we do things that are morally in line with the teaching of God. On the other hand, we struggle daily with actions and thoughts that go against the teaching of the Word of God. This is when we need to cast down our arguments and replace *"every high thing that exalts itself against the knowledge of God, bringing every thought into captivity to the obedience of Christ"* (2 Corinthians 10:5, NKJV). We are actually replacing our ideas with His, and applying His ways while abandoning ours.

Think Like God

Here is a simple exercise. The next time you start thinking about something negative, change that thought and instead think about something in the Word that says the opposite. This is one way to train your mind to think like God. You must affix your mind to something that's in the Word. If you start exercising yourself in this practice, you will begin to see blessing, better living, and favor come into your life. You will begin to see vineyards you didn't plant and houses you didn't build (Joshua 24:13).

When operating on a higher level in God, our actions won't always make sense to people, Christians and non-Christians alike—even saved, sanctified, and Holy Ghost-filled people—but you must be determined not to allow them to deter you from godly exercise. They may not fathom what you're doing, but remember once you start thinking like God, no one can stop you.

Be prepared to be ridiculed, ostracized, and talked about. After all, why would you expect an altar to burst into flame after throwing twelve barrels of water at it?[1] This is exactly what happened to Elijah the prophet when he had a great showdown with the false prophets on Mount Carmel. After watching them cut themselves and throw themselves on the altar for hours trying to get their god to answer them, Elijah called upon the name of the Lord and the altar of God, which after being drenched with water became consumed by the fire of God. Anybody looking at Elijah would have thought he had lost his mind, but Elijah knew enough about God that he had all confidence that God would and could do the ridiculous. There's no way Elijah would have attempted this if he hadn't first captured the thoughts of God.

We must realize that everything we see in the world came out of the mind of God, including all things *"that are in heaven and that are on earth, visible and invisible, whether thrones or dominions or principalities or powers. All things were created through Him and for Him"* (Colossians 1:16). We must understand that whenever God thinks and speaks, something comes into being. Anything we ask in faith is already in Him. This is the level of command we want to attain. Elijah called down fire from heaven, Joshua stopped the earth's rotation when he commanded the sun to stand still, and the walls of Jericho fell with one shout.

Can we think like God while living in the earthly realm? I certainly think we can. Our new birth in Christ provides the mechanics to think like

---

1 See I Kings 18.

Him. The scripture says, *"And you hath he quickened, who were dead in trespasses and sins"* (Ephesians 2:1). In other words, we are now made alive to the things of God. Of course, as a newborn babe in Christ you aren't going to come into certain truths right away. But you have the tools and have been made aware of the things of God.

Jesus said, *"Learn of me"* (Matthew 11:29). It's going to take a learning process. In learning the Word of God, your mind can begin to capture the thoughts of God.

My first birth, or my natural birth, wired me to think like a man. It equipped me with the human proclivities I needed to survive on this planet. My natural proclivities came from my progenitor, Adam. Adam's DNA is in me; therefore, I think and behave like Adam.

My new birth in Christ Jesus endowed me with the nature of God Himself. Now I have within me not only my human tendencies, but also God's tendencies. The transformation of my mind will put me in touch with the God inside me, and eventually His goodness and tendencies will outshine mine.

Paul the Apostle said, *"I die daily"* (1 Corinthians 15:31). I die so that Christ can come alive in me. I can then join with Paul and say,

> *I have been crucified with Christ and I no longer live, but Christ lives in me. The life I now live in the body, I live by faith in the Son of God, who loved me and gave himself for me.*
>
> —Galatians 2:20, NIV

Genesis tells us that man was made in the likeness and similitude of God. God gave him dominion over the works of His hands. All that Adam knew was taught to him by God; God was his only source of intellect. His cognitive functions were placed in him by God and no other.

When Adam named the birds, the animals and so on, God agreed with him. God only agreed with Adam because the names he gave the creatures were the same names God had given them before the world existed. If Adam had given them names God did not have in mind, He would not have endorsed him. This is proof that when God breathed the breath of life into Adam, He also gave him His mind. The first cognitive function Adam had came from God. In other words, Adam was thinking the exact things God was thinking. That made him a God-thinker.

Before the devil showed up in Genesis 3, the only opinion that existed was God's. The only way of thinking was God's. During this time, everything was blissful and peaceful in the garden God had provided for the wellbeing and survival of man. When only God's thoughts prevailed, the very earth, moon, and stars—everything on the earth and beneath it—were in alignment with the thoughts of God.

The Other Thought Process

When Adam and Eve disobeyed, they rejected God's thoughts and obeyed the thoughts presented by the devil. After that, man was no longer the image of God. All he had left was his own intellect. He was trapped because of what the devil had taught him. When he obeyed the devil's ideas and refused to think like God, he started thinking like the devil. All it took was a thought. Thus began the battle between what God said versus what the devil said.

Satan's opinion became the second way of thinking, and of course we know what happened when Adam and Eve bought into that thought process. Satan's way of thinking was in direct opposition to God's. His opinion led to self-will and a wisdom that is sensual and destructive. We are warned that the devil's intentions are evil, and therefore his thoughts towards us are not good. The Bible tells us that his only purpose is to steal, kill, and destroy (John 10:10).

Satan could only defeat Adam after he disarmed him of God's way of thinking, for it is totally impossible for Satan to destroy us or rob us of our destiny if we keep the Word of God in us. We must hide God's Word in our heart so that we will not sin against Him (Psalm 119:11). We must do everything in our power to ensure that His Word is always present in our minds. This was so important that God told the Israelites that the words He had given them should be kept in their hearts. This wasn't a question or a choice, but a command. And not only were they to keep it in their hearts, they were to ensure that it remains in the minds of their children:

Capturing the Thoughts of God

And thou shalt teach them diligently unto thy children, and shalt talk of them when thou sittest in thine house, and when thou walkest by the way, and when thou liest down, and when thou risest up. And thou shalt bind them for a sign upon thine hand, and they shall be as frontlets between thine eyes.

—Deuteronomy 6:7–8

By keeping His Word in their hearts and constantly on their mind, God was making sure that they would capture His mind. Anything outside of that would give space to the devil.

The Bible explicitly states that *"the carnal mind is enmity against God: for it is not subject to the law of God, neither indeed can be"* (Romans 8:7). The New International Version breaks it down this way: *"The mind governed by the flesh is hostile to God; it does not submit to God's law, nor can it do so"* (NIV). The carnal mind puts us on the side of the world and causes us to think and act like the world. It is unrealistic to have Kingdom expectations with a carnal mind. The things of the Kingdom won't come into our lives simply because of our church membership or our longevity in ministry. We will gain the things of the Kingdom when we become spiritually minded, for *"to be spiritually minded is life and peace"* (Romans 8:6).

Capturing the thoughts of God therefore can only be accomplished when our minds are mature. Maturity, in this sense, has nothing to do with age; it refers to one who can identify God's thoughts versus the devil's. Of course, living in a sinful world makes this a challenge. In order for us to begin this journey, we must first be ready to accept our God's unorthodox ways. His way of doing things doesn't always match what we think should be done or how we think it should be done.

Just think of the journey God put Joseph on. God needed a man in Egypt to save His people from an upcoming famine. Having someone in the Egyptian kingdom would be an effective way of saving Israel. This plan seemed perfect, but instead of simply placing Joseph on a camel and sending him to Egypt, Joseph was hated by his brothers, thrown into a pit, sold into slavery, lied about by Potiphar's wife, and put into prison—all before he was elevated to a leadership position in Egypt. If Joseph hadn't been familiar with God, he could have lost faith and given in to temptations. The end of his story would have been drastically different (Genesis 37—41). God's thoughts for Joseph were revealed to him in a dream when He showed him His plans to elevate him above everyone, including his family. Joseph's love for his God was in the back of his mind, which enabled him to go through what he did with dignity. Imagine what we could withstand if God's thoughts were predominant in our minds.

We've already identified that the Bible contains God's thoughts, so it goes without saying that to capture God's thoughts we must have a love for the Word of God. We must be consistent in reading the Word. God's Word is God, and if we have exposed ourselves to His Word, we have exposed ourselves to the mind of God.

Jesus said, *"These are the very Scriptures that testify about me"* (John 5:39, NIV). The Word gives us insight into who God is and how He thinks. We must therefore pursue the Word of God passionately if we really want to know who God is and how He thinks. Paul said, *"Let the word of Christ dwell in you richly..."* (Colossians 3:16). Remember, the Word of God gives us insight into the mind of God, so if the Word dwells in us, it is natural that we're going to start thinking like God.

Have you noticed that when you study a particular subject in school, your thought process changes so much that you begin to interpret various aspects of life in the context of what you've studied? Likewise, when the Word of God dwells in us richly, we will start to interpret the events of our lives in the context of the Word. When we begin to see life and different situations in the context of the Word, we will have captured the thoughts of God. We will be on our way to thinking like God.

chapter three
HOW DOES GOD THINK?

How does God think? We know this:

For my thoughts are not your thoughts, neither are your ways my ways, saith the Lord. For as the heavens are higher than the earth, so are my ways higher than your ways, and my thoughts than your thoughts.
—Isaiah 55:8–9

The statement is clear: God doesn't think like us, and His thoughts are above ours. No matter how wise we are, no matter what level of education we have, no matter how much street smarts we gain, God's thoughts are greater than ours. As a matter of fact, the Bible tells us that *"the wisdom of this world is foolishness with God"* (I Corinthians 3:19). The greatest philosopher can never gain enough information to match or outsmart our God. He is all-knowing. This is why many scientists don't believe in the existence of God. They're constantly looking for a tangible way to disprove the existence of God.

Genesis 1:3 says, *"And God said, Let there be light."* God's thoughts are powerful and effective. The earth and the sea, birds and animals, the trees and plants, everything began in the thoughts of God. Everything He spoke in Genesis was already in His blueprint.

Nothing ever "just happens" where God is concerned. Some of man's greatest inventions were invented through accidental discoveries. Not with God. Whatever He thinks, speaks, and commands will come into being. Some of us can attest to the fact that we have had great ideas—at least, they seemed great in our minds. But due to limited resources or intelligence, we were unable to see those ideas fulfilled. God, on the other hand, needs no assistance. He thinks, He speaks, and it is done.

Is it possible to know how God thinks? Yes, it is. God has revealed Himself to us through His words and actions, which are documented in the Bible and through His spirit.

> *For what man knoweth the things of a man, save the spirit of man which is in him? even so the things of God knoweth no man, but the Spirit of God.*
> —I Corinthians 2:11

Thoughts Revealed through His Word

After Adam and Eve were expelled from the Garden of Eden, God continued to communicate with mankind. Whether it was through signs like a burning bush, a rainbow, direct theophany, or prophets, God never wanted to hide from His creation. The prophets often told the people when God was pleased or displeased with what they did or didn't do.

Throughout this process, God was revealing His character and thoughts to mankind. If you think about it, the only way to know someone's thoughts is to listen to them speak. Luke 6:45 says,

> *A good man out of the good treasure of his heart bringeth forth that which is good; and an evil man out of the evil treasure of his heart bringeth forth that which is evil: for of the abundance of the heart his mouth speaketh.*

It's impossible to separate someone's action from their thoughts. Solomon, in his wisdom, proclaims that whatever a man thinks in his heart, that is what he is (Proverbs 23:7). We are what we think. No matter how we try to hide it or pretend, our thoughts are eventually exposed through what we say and do. Therefore, if we listen to what God says in His Word or what He whispers in our hearts, we can know God's thoughts.

What God reveals about Himself is true: *"God is not a man, that he should lie"* (Numbers 23:19). There is no pretense or falsehood in God. His attributes cannot be separated from who He is or what He thinks. He not only loves, but He *is* love, and therefore His thoughts are filled with love.

How Does God Think?

For God so loved the world, that he gave his only begotten son...

—John 3:16

Being privy to the present and future wickedness of the world, the omniscient God should have executed judgment instead of devising a plan to save mankind—that is, if His thoughts were anything but good towards us. What else could He have been thinking while He stood accused before Pilate? What else could He have been thinking while He was being stripped and whipped? What else could He have been thinking while He hung on the cross?

I can assure you, if it was me in that position, I wouldn't have been thinking peace or love. As a matter of fact, my thoughts for those responsible for placing me on the cross would have been filled with anger and hatred. But His thoughts are not my thoughts.

His Thoughts Toward Man

Throughout the Bible, God has revealed His thoughts towards man:

For I know the thoughts that I think toward you, saith the Lord, thoughts of peace, and not of evil, to give you an expected end.

—Jeremiah 29:11

What is man, that thou art mindful of him? and the son of man, that thou visitest him?

—Psalms 8:4

God's love for mankind has never changed. From the installation of the Old Testament's sacrificial order to the New Testament's baptism, God has put in place a plan for man's redemption.

Jesus told the parable of the prodigal son, which resonates with His thoughts towards us. In this parable, a man had two sons, and the younger prematurely decided to take his inheritance, leave home, and spend riotously it. When he had nothing left, he returned home thinking that he would have to renounce his position as a son and beg for forgiveness. To his surprise, his father did the opposite; his father didn't care that he was dirty and smelly, but was overjoyed that his son, who had once been lost, was found.

After seeing the condition of his son, the father probably said to himself, *I cannot let anyone see my son this way.* So he called for his best robe to cover him. Not only that, but he called for his ring, which reaffirmed him as his son. He even put shoes on his son's feet. The father could have turned his back, but his love for his son was so great that it didn't matter what he had done. His thoughts toward his son were of love, sympathy, forgiveness, and restoration, which were demonstrated in his actions. This represents God's thoughts towards us.

In another incident, the Pharisees brought a woman to Jesus who had been caught in the act of adultery. Jesus didn't interrogate her. He didn't side with the accusers (although some had been actual witnesses). Instead He was moved with compassion. The omniscient God knew the truth and yet was willing to overlook her faults. What did He think of her? Perhaps He thought, *Yes, you are guilty. Yes, the law says you should die. Yes, there were witnesses. But my thoughts of you are of restoration. I want you to have peace. Whatever brought you to this point in your life, I forgive you.*

God's love and compassion for us isn't based on what we've done or who we are. His thoughts are righteous and just:

> *He is the Rock, his work is perfect: for all his ways are judgment: a God of truth and without iniquity, just and right is he.*
> —Deuteronomy 32:4

In a world where the lines of right and wrong are blurred and everyone conforms to societal pressures, God never changes. His thoughts are righteous no matter the situation or era.

We never have to worry that God's thoughts will become evil or unfair. When we find ourselves in a situation that isn't in line with His principles, we can rest assured that He won't judge us or make assumptions based on what others have said. He cannot be swayed by the masses. He is no respecter of persons.

How many times have we made judgments about someone without knowing both sides of the story? We become the judge, jury, and executioner

How Does God Think?

with limited and sometimes bias information. But that isn't how God thinks. He will always move in righteousness, justice, and love.

Don't get me wrong: God doesn't tolerate or accept sin. Hebrews 12:6 says that He chastens everyone whom He loves. His correction isn't an indication that His thoughts towards us have changed; neither does He react based on what we did. His intent isn't to see us hurt, but rather to ensure that we come into the fullness of His plan for us. His Word declares, *"For he hath made him to be sin for us, who knew no sin; that we might be made the righteousness of God in him"* (2 Corinthians 5:21). Once we put on the name of Jesus, He no longer sees us as lawbreakers or sinful; through Him, we become righteous. We only need to remember that His thoughts towards us are *"of peace, and not of evil"* (Jeremiah 29:11), repent before Him, and move forward.

It has been revealed that God's attributes are a reflection of His thoughts. Can you imagine what we could learn if we would only explore the Word of God and open our hearts to His spirit? We can know what God thinks!

chapter four
EXAMINING OUR LIMITATIONS

WHY ARE WE SO WEAK? COULD IT BE BECAUSE WE'RE OPERATING BENEATH OUR God-given potential? What do we have to do to position ourselves on the earth the way God intended?

From the beginning, we see the weakness of man. Adam and Eve had an ideal life in the Garden of Eden, living in a sin-free environment. After the fall, they fell into a downward spiral. When sin entered the world, it rendered everyone born of a woman weak and corrupt. We are thus sinful from birth. As the psalmist states, *"Surely I was sinful at birth, sinful from the time my mother conceived me"* (Psalm 51:5, NIV). This is the nature we are born with.

Because of our sinful nature, we don't naturally abide by the will or laws of God. The Bible calls our sinful nature depraved. It is this nature that caused the prophet Jerimiah to write, *"The heart is deceitful above all things and beyond cure"* (Jeremiah 17:9, NIV).

However, now that we've decided to follow Jesus and build our lives around Him, our nature needs to change. Although we seek to do His will—to be an example and ambassador for Him—our human nature stands in the way. Jesus said to Peter, *"The spirit is willing, but the flesh is weak"* (Matthew 26:41, NIV).

Our desire to do the will of God and live a righteous life is genuine and not pretentious. Most of us truly desire to live a life about which God can say, *"Well done, good and faithful servant!"* (Matthew 25:21, NIV) We would love to know that God is able to boast about us like He did of Job: *"Hast thou considered my servant Job, that there is none like him in the earth, a perfect and an upright man, one that feareth God, and escheweth evil?"* (Job 1:8)

Examining Our Limitations

We often find ourselves in situations, conversations, and places we know we shouldn't be in, but we are unable to leave or stop what we're doing. It's not because we want to continue in our sin. It's that we find it hard to go against our flesh. Our sinful nature often makes it difficult for us to do what is right. We are drawn into the things we want to stay away from because of our human and sinful desires. We are thus hindered from stepping out and saying, "I will not do this thing and sin against my God."

We fail to subject our human nature, thoughts, and proclivities to the will of God. Paul's writings to the Romans reveal this fight:

> *For that which I do I allow not: for what I would, that do I not; but what I hate, that do I... Now then it is no more I that do it, but sin that dwelleth in me. For I know that in me (that is, in my flesh,) dwelleth no good thing: for to will is present with me; but how to perform that which is good I find not. For the good that I would I do not: but the evil which I would not, that I do. Now if I do that I would not, it is no more I that do it, but sin that dwelleth in me. I find then a law, that, when I would do good, evil is present with me. For I delight in the law of God after the inward man: but I see another law in my members, warring against the law of my mind, and bringing me into captivity to the law of sin which is in my members. O wretched man that I am! who shall deliver me from the body of this death?*
>
> —Romans 7:15, 17–24

We are slaves to the sin. We were born in sin and shaped in iniquity. Sin is a part of us. It is engrained in our beings and we unwillingly serve this master, causing us to go against the spirit of God. Paul isn't saying that we aren't responsible for the things we do, but he definitely knows that we cannot overcome the limitations of the flesh without the power of God.

Although our sinful human nature creates challenges for us, we must continue to live and carry out our human and spiritual functions. Living for God would be easier if we didn't exist in a world that encouraged our sinful tendencies. The world's ideologies have influenced our minds so much that we find it difficult at times to distinguish between worldly principles and Kingdom principles.

Think Like God

It's not always easy to think the way God thinks, because we are heavily influenced by the world. Now that Christ is within us, we experience a constant conflict between our minds and His mind—our way of doing things and His way of doing things. And now that Christ is in us, we experience a constant inner battle between the things of the flesh and the things of the spirit. The apostle Paul puts it this way: *"For the flesh lusteth against the Spirit, and the Spirit against the flesh: and these are contrary the one to the other: so that ye cannot do the things that ye would"* (Galatians 5:17). It is a battle between His mind and our mind, our way of doing things versus His way of doing things.

The Christ in us didn't remove our human nature. If we're going to fulfill our purpose on the earth and move beyond our human limitations, we must battle every day of our lives with gritted teeth and determination to bring our thoughts and lives under the subjection of Christ.

The human way of thinking is very limited. If we're going to think like God, we must recognize that His thoughts and ways are beyond our human reasoning. But how do we think outside of ourselves or beyond what we can comprehend? The Bible says, *"Let no man deceive himself. If any man among you seemeth to be wise in this world, let him become a fool, that he may be wise. For the wisdom of this world is foolishness with God"* (1 Corinthians 3:18–19).

The mind that is trained in the wisdom of this world is only good for the things of this world. It is obvious that our belief and acceptance of this world cannot qualify us to be God thinkers. This is why some of the most brilliant minds in our society don't believe in God and cannot explain the simplest things about the very God who gave them breath.

Man's brilliance and intelligence cannot fathom God. There will always be a battle between humanity and His divinity, between man-ness and God-ness, between man's thoughts and God's thoughts. To master the God-way of thinking, we have to be ready to count everything we've accomplished and desired as nothing. Paul the Apostle said it this way: *"I count all things but loss for the excellency of the knowledge of Christ Jesus my Lord: for whom I have suffered the loss of all things, and do count them but dung, that I may win Christ"* (Philippians 3:8).

Examining Our Limitations

The Five Giants: Our Senses

Even when we know Jesus Christ, we find it easier to work with our natural tendencies, trapped in the confines of our five senses. We need our five senses to survive in this life, but we also find that our senses, when it comes to matters of faith, become giants to overcome. Although they are important to us, they can become our greatest enemy. Faith says, "We must abandon our senses to relate to things unseen." But our flesh says: "That's impossible." God's way of thinking says, "Sorry, you can't use your senses right now." Our senses say, "We were here first and we will not be silenced." The battle goes on and on.

How do we comprehend that which we cannot see? How do we explain that which we cannot touch? How do we touch what we cannot feel, for God is spirit and therefore invisible? How do we taste and smell that which has no physical form? If our senses cannot make a connection to an invisible God, then it is easy for us to conclude that He doesn't exist. Even if we believe He exists, how do we explain that which is beyond the scope of our senses? How do we explain the unseen to those who rely on what they see for proof? He must first become real to us by faith. We must see proof at some point in our faith walk. Faith without immediate proof is for believers, yet there are times when even believers need proof. Acts 1:3 says, *"To whom also he shewed himself alive after his passion by many infallible proofs, being seen of them forty days, and speaking of the things pertaining to the kingdom of God."* God will be better explained when we, through our faith, begin to experience the reality of His person and presence in our lives.

Our Desires

Not only is it important to rule over our senses, we must also be in control of desires that are aroused from what we see, hear, smell, taste, or touch. Giving into our human desires often limits us from becoming who we ought to be in God. Wanting to do what is right and actually doing what is right are two different things. Our human desires, more often than not, lead us to satisfy our earthly needs and wants.

Think Like God

The writer of Ephesians said that before we became children of God, we lived *"gratifying the cravings of our flesh and following its desires and thoughts. Like the rest, we were by nature deserving of wrath"* (Ephesians 2:3, NIV). We sought after the things that made us feel good and stroked our ego. We chased after things that satisfied our passions—or, as the Apostle Paul called it, the "works of the flesh"—thus making us worthy of the wrath of God. Now that we belong to God, our desires must change. We must seek the things that please God.

Desiring godly things goes against our very nature. We don't always want to do the right thing because sin is often easier and tends to feel better than living righteously. For example, it's easier to give a harsh answer to someone who says something negative to us. However, the word of God tells us, *"A soft answer turneth away wrath: but grievous words stir up anger"* (Proverbs 15:1). In a case where someone is rude to us, the natural thing to do is lash out and defend ourselves, pacifying our flesh which says, "How dare you speak to me that way!" What we'd like to say and how we'd like to say it often goes against how God would like us to handle the situation.

We see examples throughout the Bible of what happens when we seek to fulfill our own desires. David, who was described as a man after God's own heart, lost his child because he was overcome by his lust for Bathsheba. In an attempt to cover his wrongdoings, he had her husband killed (2 Samuel 11–18). Ananias and Sapphira lost their lives because of pride and greed when they lied to the Holy Spirit about the profit made from the sale of their property (Acts 5:1–11). Saul lost the kingdom when he disobeyed God and held back the best of the captives for himself because of a selfish desire (1 Samuel 15:1–35). Judas betrayed our Lord and Savior for thirty pieces of silver to satisfy his love of money (Matthew 26:15). Can you imagine being in the presence of Jesus, walking and talking with Him, observing and participating in the miracles He performed, and still allowing your human desire to overpower you? Greed, self-promotion, and lust will lead you away from the mind of God. We can never reach our potential in God and think like God if we don't align our desires with God's desires.

In other words, our human desires and proclivities cause us to go after the wrong things and prevent us from seeking God. If we don't constantly keep our fleshy desires in check, we will always succumb to them. We have to make a conscious effort to ensure our human desires don't mold our actions.

Examining Our Limitations

Our Emotions

Our desires aren't the only things engrained in our nature that restrict our ability to be like God. Our emotions also prohibit us from moving towards God.

As humans, we're emotional beings. God made us this way. Most of our responses and actions are initiated by our emotions. If you're a parent, you probably remember when you held your child for the first time—or saw them take their first steps or graduate from high school. The feeling of joy that flows over you is overwhelming and makes you want to tell everyone. These great feelings of euphoria can cause a parent to overlook things another person might not.

On the other hand, the gravity of sadness we feel at the loss of a loved one can leave us in pain. The emotional strain caused by difficult situations renders us weak. Think of a time when you were emotional about something, whether you were angry, sad, jealous, or confused. How clearly were you able to think? How strong were your feelings? Being emotional makes us vulnerable and unable to think logically—or spiritually. Therefore, our emotions can limit us from doing the will of God when we allow them to overtake us.

Take Cain, for example. Unlike his parents, who knew the safety of the garden, he had to grapple with jealousy and anger. Cain, like his brother Abel, knew the process of giving sacrifices to God. He knew that he was to offer the best sacrifice to God, and yet he didn't. When God told Cain He wasn't happy with his sacrifice, *"Cain was very wroth, and his countenance fell"* (Genesis 4:5). It was in this state of jealousy and anger that Cain acted and killed his brother.

We often allow our emotions to get the best of us, and as a result we kill what God is doing inside of us. Our emotions cause us to say what we don't want to say. They also cause us to think and believe lies instead of God's truth.

If we are to learn the mind of God, we need to learn not to react to our emotions. Peter experienced something rare and supernatural when he walked on water, yet when fear took hold of him he began to sink, unable to see Jesus. Fear is among the most crippling emotions a Christian can experience. Although God's Word tells us that He hasn't given us the spirit of fear, but one of love and a sound mind (2 Timothy 1:7), we often lose the sound mind and our connection to God when fear and other strong emotions set in.

Think Like God

We tend to serve God best when we're in a good emotional state. We give great testimonies when we're happy, pray for others when we're content, give to the poor when we feel blessed, and spread the good news when we feel comfortable. But when the opposite is true, we sometimes fail to function in the same manner. Instead our faith becomes weak and our godly thought process blur. We can't allow our emotions to dictate and control our obedience to God. Our circumstances won't always be favorable, and they can negatively affect our emotions. We can't hinge our faith and actions on how we feel.

Jesus Himself was tempted while on the earth. He went through the same growing pains we all do. In the garden of Gethsemane, He shared His feelings with His disciples, telling them that His soul was *"exceeding sorrowful"* (Matthew 26:38). He prayed to the Father, asking, "[I]f it be possible, let this cup pass from me: nevertheless not as I will, but as thou wilt" (Matthew 26:39). If Jesus had let the sorrow of His heart rule His actions, He could have ended His prayer on that note. Instead He said, *"Nevertheless not as I will, but as thou wilt"* (Matthew 26:39). Jesus was able to get past His feelings and do the will of God.

If we know we're going to get through it, it's easier to keep our emotions in check when we're faced with unwelcome and painful situations. We need to keep our goal in mind. Scripture tells us that Jesus was able to look ahead to *"the joy that was set before him,"* and as a result He *"endured the cross, despising the shame"* (Hebrews 12:2). We are given a number of goals in Scripture to aim for in the midst of persecution and hardship. My favorite one is found in Romans 8:18: *"For I reckon that the sufferings of this present time are not worthy to be compared with the glory which shall be revealed in us."*

Our emotions can cause us to feel that we can't do the task set before us. But that's when we have to remember that there's a reason we need to overcome and that we have a God who knows what we're feeling and is able to help us through it. The writer of Hebrews takes it even further, saying,

> *For we do not have a high priest who cannot sympathize with our weaknesses, but One who has been tempted in all things as we are, yet without sin. Therefore let us draw near with confidence to the throne of grace, so that we may receive mercy and find grace to help in time of need.*
>
> —Hebrews 4:15–16, NASB

Examining Our Limitations

Can we be like Jesus? Oh yes, we can. That's what we're striving for—the mind of God.

We were born in sin and shaped in inequity. We have our father Adam's nature. We are emotional beings who are limited in many ways because of a sinful nature. Our desires are often selfish and overpowering. So how can we win? How can we overcome this fleshy nature and be the man or woman God wants us to be?

Seek for the mind of God! Start thinking like Him. The mind of God will say, "Although I see the storm around me, I can still walk on the water. Although I'm filled with sorrow, I can still do the will of God. Although I don't know what will happen tomorrow, I won't be afraid." If we can just think like God, the emotions which once guided our actions, the thoughts which can only comprehend so much, and the desires which sometimes get us in trouble will no longer limit or stop us.

We then need to ask ourselves the following questions. Whose opinion are we following? Whose thoughts are we processing? Whose desires are ruling our actions? We've already explored what happens when we follow our own human thoughts, desires, and emotions. It will never lead us to a fulfilled life in God. But blessed is a man whose *"delight is in the law of the Lord; and in his law doth he meditate day and night"* (Psalms 1:2).

The only way to identify and combat the limitations of our humanity is to acknowledge the vastness of God. We must *"[crucify] the flesh with its passions and desires"* (Galatians 5:24, NIV) in order to think like God.

If we work to seek the mind of God, we can overcome our limitations and become all that God intended us to be.

chapter five
RESTORING THE ORDER

In the beginning God created the heaven and the earth... And God saw every thing that he had made, and, behold, it was very good.

—Genesis 1:1, 31

GOD'S CREATION WAS FLAWLESS. IT WAS PERFECT AND WELL PLANNED OUT. God placed everything in order, from the separation of the light from the darkness to the herbs and trees that contained seeds after their own kind. God Himself was delighted with the outcome.

Once the atmosphere was pure and the land ready, God stooped down, created Adam from the dust of the earth, and blew into him the breath of life. He didn't just speak man into existence as He did the other creations. Man's creation was not just an afterthought. God carefully thought about it and created man in His own image. Adam was by no means a god, but his character and way of thinking was an imprint of God. As mentioned before, Adam's thought process was so much like God's that when God brought the animals before Adam to be named *"whatsoever Adam called every living creature, that was the name thereof"* (Genesis 2:19).

Not long after God created Eve as a companion for Adam, Adam and Eve lived in a garden that satisfied their physical needs—as every tree in the garden was good for food, except the tree of knowledge—and was beautiful, thus making it a pleasurable place to live (Genesis 2:9). There were no wild animals to fear, no poisonous plants to watch for. It was a place we would today consider paradise.

As wonderful as all that was, the most important aspect of the garden experience was the relationship Adam and Eve had with God. Genesis indicates that God's voice could be heard through the garden in the cool of the day, when God came and spoke with His creation. Living in an environment free from distractions, stress, and pain, they could hear the voice of God so plainly that is almost unthinkable. But that's what Adam and Eve experienced every day.

Adam and Eve lived the life that God intended us to live, until that dreadful day when Eve entertained the devil's conversation. The fall not only caused a catastrophic change in the earthly realm, but also the relationship between God and man. Death, spiritual and physical, entered into the equation and the human race had to deal with it. Man was no longer innocent and his mind was no longer pure and godlike. As time went on, man's mind became so corrupt that when God looked at man, He *"saw that the wickedness of man was great in the earth, and that every imagination of the thoughts of his heart was only evil continually"* (Genesis 6:5).

I wonder what the world would be like if Adam and Eve hadn't sinned? I truly believe the world would be like the Garden of Eden. Imagine, finding peace and tranquility everywhere you went in this world. A place where with no murderers, no evil, and no sickness. You could go where you wanted without fear or concern. You would feel the presence of God at all times and hear His voice communing with you. Your thoughts would be in sync with your heavenly Father's thoughts. You wouldn't question or doubt His will or desires. God's plan for the human race was for man to live forever in this state. Fear, pain, hatred, and anger was never part of the plan. You were never to experience death.

We may not be able to find the Garden of Eden in the presently evil world, but when we obey God we can find the experiences of Eden in our hearts. At creation, God's emphasis was on a place or location—the Garden. In the new creation, the emphasis is on an experience—peace and rest). As Isaiah 26:3 says, *"[God] will keep him in perfect peace, whose mind is stayed on [Him]"* (NKJV). We will find provision and relationship with God, who *"shall supply all your need according to his riches in glory"* (Philippians 4:19). As for His relationship with man, He promised that He will be with us even unto the end of the world.

The entire Edenic experience can be found in Jesus Christ. He embodied the fullness of everything God is and desires for mankind.

THINK LIKE GOD

The First Adam Versus the Second Adam

God has never abandoned the Edenic ideals. His purpose for the regeneration plan is to establish the same ideals in our lives on earth, both now and in the future.

An examination of Scripture will reveal obvious similarities between Adam and Jesus Christ. The first Adam was made a living soul; the second Adam was made a quickening spirit. The first Adam was tempted by the devil in Genesis 3; the second Adam was tempted by the devil in Matthew 4. The first Adam was tempted with food and yielded to temptation; the second Adam was tempted to command stones to be made into bread, but he overcame the temptation by using the Word. After the fall of the first Adam, God sent seraphims to guard the tree of life; after the second Adam was tempted, God sent an angel to minister to Him. God sent Jesus, the second Adam, to restore unto us what He gave the first Adam: dominion, authority, and power over the works of His hands.

We must realize that when we walk in God's Word, we are in position to continue God's original plan. On the other hand, compromising His Word to entertain man's ideology is destructive and detrimental to our relationship with God. If we compromise His Word, we give up our position and place of authority to the devil—not that the devil can occupy our position. As a matter of fact, the devil doesn't want to occupy our position, because he knows he cannot. But that does not stop him from trying to move us from where God placed us.

Satan couldn't occupy Adam's positon; he just wanted him out of position. Why? Because Adam bore the likeness of God and was Satan's greatest threat on the earth. Satan must have known that Adam was the progenitor of the human race. He knew that if he could persuade Adam to sin, the future of humanity would be in great danger. We shouldn't be ignorant of the devil's devices (2 Corinthians 2:11). We must be aware that he's not just after the head of the house; he wants the whole house. The reason he is so intense in striking the shepherd is that he knows if he gets the shepherd, the sheep will scatter (Mark 14:27).

Restoring the Order

Temptation

This brings us to the topic of temptation. Temptation is never about the person or the situation; the devil is always after something bigger. He tries to mess us up before we can reach our potential, stopping us before we obtain our goal. He isn't interested in where we are now, but where we're going. He knows how to destroy our tomorrow, today.

Nobody gets to significance without first bearing the mark of insignificance. Nobody gets to greatness without first bearing the mark of smallness. We must therefore bear in mind that the moment of temptation is always about something else. When we examine the temptation of Jesus in the wilderness, we see that Jesus, after His forty-day fast, addressed the devil's enticement. In Matthew 4:3, the devil said to Jesus, *"If thou be the Son of God, command that these stones be made bread."* On the surface, it appears the temptation was only about the bread and the stones, but it was more about the Sonship of Jesus. The devil's questions were very strategic; if Jesus had turned the stones into bread, He would have obeyed the tempter and everyone would have said that the devil had conquered Jesus. This, of course, would have jeopardized His Sonship, for He could never be God if he had succumbed to the devil's temptation.

I won't go into detail about the power of sonship, but I will implore you to not allow the devil to take your sonship from you. Sonship means that you have God's DNA. If you think about it for a moment, you'll understand why the devil is trying his best to remove us from our position and place of authority through temptation. If Adam hadn't subjected himself to the temptation, Satan wouldn't have the power he has on earth.

You and I are Satan's greatest nightmare on earth. When we resist him, he flees from us. Yes, we, mortal beings, resist the devil and he flees. He takes off in a hurry! What is it about us that causes this enemy to run? The Bible says that it takes just one of us to chase a thousand; two of us can *"put ten thousand to flight"* (Deuteronomy 32:30). The prophet Elijah told his servant, *"Those who are with us are more than those who are with them"* (2 Kings 6:16). When God's people shout, walls fall down. We are the giants of the land, not the sons of the Anakim (Deuteronomy 9:2). We are greater, not the politicians, not the millionaires. We are! He gave *us* the power to bind and loose in the earth, not them. We are the ones with the Kingdom of God in us.

There is a vast difference between appearance and reality. This's why we must never forget that the devil is a liar. Everything he does and says is a lie. When he shows up, don't believe him. Believe what God has said, for He's the real deal.

At Adam's disobedience, the whole creation turned upside-down. Everything went wild. As previously mentioned, before Adam's disobedience there were no wild animals, no venomous snakes or killer whales. The curse God pronounced on the earth affected not only humans but the animal kingdom as well. Adam didn't have to cage the lions and tigers because man was in position to reign over the works of God's hand. The prophet Isaiah wrote,

> *The wolf also shall dwell with the lamb, and the leopard shall lie down with the kid; and the calf and the young lion and the fatling together; and a little child shall lead them. And the cow and the bear shall feed; their young ones shall lie down together: and the lion shall eat straw like the ox. And the sucking child shall play on the hole of the asp, and the weaned child shall put his hand on the cockatrice' den. They shall not hurt nor destroy in all my holy mountain: for the earth shall be full of the knowledge of the Lord, as the waters cover the sea.*
>
> —Isaiah 11:6–9

Jesus came to earth to restore the order to the way God intended it to be from the beginning. I find it hard to believe that God would allow the devil to disrupt His order and do nothing about it. His coming was definitely to restore order, and to reposition His people over the works of His hand.

Many of us are looking to the future for this to happen, but the restoration started the very day Jesus was born in a manger. The devil knew this and raised up Herod to kill all the baby boys, hoping to also kill Jesus (Matthew 2:16). This is intriguing, because the same action was seen in Egypt in the days of the exodus, when the authorities ordered the death of little baby boys, not so much because they were afraid of them but because they were afraid of what they would become. Let me say this again: the devil isn't interested in who you are now; he is scared of who you are about to become.

Restoring the Order

Somehow King Herod must have known his days were numbered, for the real king was here. Satan had raised him up to destroy Jesus, but there was no plan great enough to stop Him. God cannot be defeated. Neither does He accept defeat. The birth of Jesus Christ was His way of saying that it's time to restore order.

Man was made in the image of God. Whenever Adam spoke or acted, he mirrored God. In other words, he did and said the things God would have done and said. Man had no image of himself. He had no portrait of himself; he only reflected who God was. It was the devil who introduced to them self-consciousness. He introduced *"the lust of the eyes, and the pride of life"* (I John 2:16). They exchanged their place in God to be like gods. What a tragedy!

The truth of the matter is that we cannot disobey God without giving up something. Reuben defiled his father's bed and lost his inheritance. Esau sold his birthright for one morsel of meat and found no place of repentance, though he sought it carefully with tears. Before we make decisions, we should take note of what we have to give up or what it is we have to lose in order to gain. Adam gave up the image of his God to be like gods. How depressing and sad this narrative is.

God had to defend Himself. I know He did it because He loved the world, but can you imagine what would have happened if God had refused to do something about the chaos the devil inflicted on His creation? The devil would have had a perpetual party. God couldn't allow this to happen, so it was necessary for Christ Jesus, the image of the invisible God, the firstborn of every creature, the brightness of His glory and the express image of His person, to become the hope of glory.

In other words, the image that man lost when he sinned was found in Christ Jesus, and the same Christ Jesus who bears the radiance of God resides in me. What other conclusion can we come to than Jesus came to restore us to the likeness of God and to put His people in charge of the works of His hands? We need to grab a hold of this fact. Not only do we have human tendencies, but we have God-like tendencies as well. We can do God things, because that which was stolen from Adam is given back to us through the indwelling of Christ Jesus in our bodies. Everything the devil stole from the first Adam, Jesus Christ, the second Adam, came to give it back to us.

Think Like God

We must understand that the church is God's headquarters on earth. As long as we're here, we have a say about what goes on, when it goes on, and where it goes on. The Bible says that *"[w]hen the righteous are in authority, the people rejoice: but when the wicked beareth rule, the people mourn"* (Proverbs 29:2). We shouldn't ignore the world we live in. Why should we leave it up to the wicked when we are the restored ones? There is a song that says, "Sons of God arise, sons of God arise." We need to arise and take back our place in God. We are the light and salt of the earth. We are still relevant in the name of Jesus. We cannot rule from the position of the kingdom of the world.

We have the power to come together in fasting and prayer as one people and demand changes. The Esther method of changing the politics of her time was for the Jewish nation to fast. She changed the political system that was aligned against them. The church, the restored ones, need to come together in fasting and prayer so the ruling powers of the earth will recognize the power of God and the church on the earth.

We rule from God's headquarters, the church. We were placed here not only to remain within the four walls of a building, but to inspire change. We are the Abrahams who stand between God and Sodom, to plead with God for the people. We are the Joshuas who speak to the sun and stops the gravitational pull on the earth. We are the Elijahs who shut up the rainclouds for three years and then loose them at the end of the fixed time. We have in us the express image of God—that is to say, we can do God things. The doings of God must be evident on the earth through us.

Yes, we have sinned and fallen short of the glory of God (Romans 3:23), but we are now complete in Him (Colossians 2:10). I Corinthians 6:11 says that we are washed and sanctified. The Bible says, *"For he hath made him to be sin for us, who knew no sin; that we might be made the righteousness of God in him"* (2 Corinthians 5:21).

There are so many scriptures describing our restored state. It is important to notice that none of them suggest or even hint that we are restored by our own efforts. We are not to maintain our restored position by our own doing. It is impossible for a man, whose DNA is contaminated with sin, to live a godly life by his own efforts. If we are going to impact our lives and the lives of others, it is necessary for us to change our physiology.

As mentioned before, it is not about how good we are or how we were raised. I have come to realize that one of the greatest hindrances in preventing the flow of the spirit of God in our lives is self-righteousness. Let me put it this way: you are not more righteous than a fornicator or an adulterer because you've never fornicated or committed adultery. I'm not advocating for immorality; I believe what the Bible says on that subject. I may not be guilty of any of the above mentioned sins, but that doesn't make me more righteous than someone else or more qualified to deal with God than the other person. My dealings with God can never be based on my merits. If it was about merits, grace would be useless.

My abstinence from sin is a good thing, but it doesn't make me righteous. There are a lot of upstanding members of society—those who are well-mannered, disciplined, faithful to their husbands and wives, and pay their taxes—who aren't saved or righteous, because righteousness cannot be attained by any other means but through Jesus Christ. It is He who transferred His righteousness unto us by the shedding of His precious blood. This was explicitly seen when Adam and Eve covered themselves with fig leaves. God then sewed for them a covering of skin—meaning that God had to kill something, and if he killed something, then blood was shed. This confirms that without the shedding of blood, there is no remission of sin (Hebrews 9:22).

Maintaining a Restored Life

To maintain a restored life, I must will myself to walk in the knowledge of who God said I am and not allow myself to fall victim to the vicissitudes of life. I must change my psychology. I cannot allow my failures to displace me from the mindset that I am the righteousness of God.

The Word of God isn't right because I do right. The opposite is also true. The Word of God isn't invalid because I do wrong. The Word of God is authentic, valid, and current when I am in the right or the wrong. Therefore, I must will my mind to stand in the reality of how God sees me, not my view of myself or others.

I'm not suggesting that we should live carelessly and recklessly. Paul asked, *"Shall we continue in sin that grace may abound? God forbid"* (Romans 6:1–2).

Think Like God

I've seen too many gifted Christians become victims of their circumstances because they didn't know how to handle their shortcomings. If you're in a pit and you forget who God says you are, you'll take on a mindset that matches our circumstances. We weren't called to walk in the likeness of our circumstances; we were called to walk in the likeness of God.

My intention here is to arm you. I will boldly say that you are the righteousness of God. Even with all the bad things you may have done since you became saved? Yes, you are the righteousness of God. If the devil can keep that knowledge from you because of your mistakes, you will never get out of where you are.

Jonah found himself in the whale's belly, but in his mind's eye he was still able to look towards the holy temple. He finally ended up where he was looking. God commanded the whale to vomit him out. If you keep looking where you are, you'll end up stuck in that place instead of getting where you want to go. If your life is in a bad place, study the rightness of God's Word. I guarantee that you'll end up where you're looking.

You are restored regardless of what's going on in your life right now. You are who God say you are, regardless of what people say. Now get up and start living that way. Resurrection power is in you. You are capable, and you are able to do more than you think you can.

God has enabled you to initiate changes. Don't let what you see and feel destroy what God has placed in you. He said that He's given us the power to become sons of God. The prodigal son was still a son, regardless of where he went (Luke 15:11–32). Every day you get up, speak into the atmosphere, "I am restored. I am who God says I am. I can, I will, and I shall come out. I can do all things through Christ who strengthens me!"

chapter six
TWO WORLDS

THE MENTION OF TWO WORLDS MAY SOUND TO SOME LIKE A PLOT DETAIL OUT OF a science fiction movie—our minds may naturally go to a show where we've seen aliens attacking Earth—but I'm not talking about a fictional world or some make-believe trip to Mars. It's a world as real as the world we live in. For every Christian, the existence of the spiritual world must be a reality.

God told us in His Word that we should seek first the Kingdom of God. In other words, He has invited us to be part of this (Kingdom or the world). The word *seek* denotes a diligent searching. As a Christian, this quest should be our first act. Above all, above all our worldly pursuits and possessions, we must learn to adapt to this new world.

Believe it or not, we were made to function in two worlds: the physical world (the kingdom of man) and the spiritual world (the Kingdom of God). There are definite differences between these worlds. The most obvious one is physical, and the other is spiritual.

It is, of course, easier to relate to the physical world than the spiritual. We have been taught since infancy how to live in this world. We've learned to breathe, to cry when we need attention or assistance, and eventually to take care of ourselves. Through the guidance of our parents, teachers, friends, and peers, we gain knowledge about the physical world.

But just as we have learned to live in this world, we also need to learn the ways of the Kingdom of God. Similarly, if I relocate to a new country after living in Canada all my life, I must learn the ways of the place I now call home. I must take the time to learn the laws of the land if I want to remain a law-abiding citizen. I need to study the roads, the street names, and the signs if I want to be able to get around without a guide. I must learn the language to ensure I can communicate with the natives of the country. I cannot say to myself, "I will do things like I did in Canada." If so, I may end up missing out on the benefits of my new home.

Likewise, now that we're part of the Kingdom of God, we must take the time needed to understand how to live in this world. There are some things we haven't tapped into because we aren't familiar with Kingdom ways. Our understanding of how things work in the physical world hinges on logic and experiences. But as we will see later, logic doesn't work in the spiritual world. As a matter of fact, the laws and principles of this new world defy logic. The things we have learned to do to survive in the physical world cannot be used in the new world. We must challenge ourselves to break free from our old perceptions, concepts, and ways of thinking if we truly want to be a part of the new world.

The principles that govern the two worlds are vastly different. The principles of this world says that our education, background, and status will define who we are and how we are treated by our peers. But the spiritual world, the Kingdom of God, is no respecter of persons (James 2:1). In other words, it doesn't matter who we are in this world, in the Kingdom of God we are a child of the King (Galatians 3:26). My last name doesn't change that. We can be the wealthiest or the poorest person, a nobody or a superstar, but in the Kingdom of God none of us are treated differently or of less importance. Galatians 3:28 tells us, *"There is neither Jew nor Greek, there is neither bond nor free, there is neither male nor female: for ye are all one in Christ Jesus."*

Our world is filled with great leaders, people with the ability to make dramatic decisions and think clearly in highly stressful situations. These leaders have made wonderful changes in this world that have contributed to the betterment of our lives. However, as great as our leaders are, they can be corrupt, evil, selfish and unconcerned. In the Kingdom of God, the ruler and maker is God. He cannot be corrupted by manipulation or blackmail.

God is always thinking about us. Scripture declares that His thoughts towards us are *"of peace, and not of evil"* (Jeremiah 29:11). So we never have to worry about the degradation of the leader's character, for He is the *"same yesterday, and to day, and for ever"* (Hebrews 13:8). Nor is He a man who will lie (Numbers 23:19); He will always do what He has said. There are no broken campaign promises.

Two Worlds

If we're going to learn about this Kingdom, we need to get close to God and submit to His authority.

In the kingdom of man, we must function and operate by what we see, feel, smell, touch, and taste. We won't do anything that doesn't make sense to us. In the spiritual world, however, our human abilities have no value; neither can we use our five senses to live and function. Seeing is believing here, but in the new world we are blessed if we believe without seeing (John 20:29).

The reason we aren't prospering in the church or excited about our lives in God is that we have it mixed up. We cannot differentiate the principles that govern the two worlds.

John 6:1–14 tells us of one of Jesus' greatest miracles. He went up to a mountain with His disciples and a multitude followed Him. After teaching them, He was moved with compassion and suggested to His disciples that they feed the multitude. Two of the disciples, Philip and Andrew, surmised the situation and saw that it was impossible. Philip responded by telling Jesus that they didn't have enough money to buy bread to feed everyone. Andrew looked around and found a boy who had five barley loaves and two small fishes. In Andrew's eyes, this could barely feed two children, much less five thousand men. The need was great, but the solutions fell short.

Both men looked at the situation from the position of the kingdom of man and therefore saw it as impossible. Once Jesus took the loaves and fishes and blessed them, He transferred them from the kingdom of man into the Kingdom of God. The little that hadn't been enough was suddenly able to feed five thousand men with an overflow, for they collected twelve baskets of leftovers! If the fish and bread remained in the hands of the lad, it would only have fed him, and maybe his father, but in the hands of Jesus great things happened. In this impossible situation, five loaves and two fishes miraculously turned into a multiplicity of loaves and fishes.

We lack many things because we don't transfer out needs into God's hands, where He can multiply them and turn them into what we need. As long as we hold things in "our" kingdom, they remain limited. They cannot multiply. But give them to God and transport them into the Kingdom of God and see what He can do.

Obedience is God's way of transferring us and what we have into the Kingdom of God. In John 2:1–11, Jesus told the disciples to fill the water pots. They obeyed and the end result was the best wine they ever had. Obedience and willingness gives us access to God's miracles of multiplicity. But we have to give God something to work with. Jesus knew the five loaves and two fishes couldn't feed the multitude, but He needed something to work with. Once the food left this kingdom and entered His Kingdom, it was no longer "little."

If the woman in Elijah's day had refused to bake a cake for the prophet, she would have destroyed not only her own wellbeing and that of her sons, but the possibility of living a prosperous life (1 Kings 17:13).

Everything you and I give to God for His service is full of possibility. It is unfortunate that sometimes we don't recognize the potential of what we have. Some of what we have is a result of what we gave to God.

> *Give, and it shall be given unto you; good measure, pressed down, and shaken together, and running over, shall men give into your bosom. For with the same measure that ye mete withal it shall be measured to you again.*
>
> —Luke 6:38

Notice that it starts with one act—giving. It's not the amount that matters, but the willingness to give, to transfer it into God's Kingdom. We'll receive everything God has for us when we are willing and obedient.

Our minds will not consider ourselves blessed if we don't have tangible evidence. We only consider ourselves blessed when we have the thing in our possession. We have to see the blessings based on what we have. We're blessed because we have the car we want or the house we longed for. But in God's economy, that logic isn't true. We're already blessed even if we don't see the fulfillment of what we prayed for.

Abraham, the faithful patriarch, was given a promise from God that a great nation and kings would come from him (Genesis 13:16, 17:6). This promise was given long before he saw its fulfillment. While he and his wife were childless, Abraham was still blessed. The Bible says, "He staggered not at the promise of God through unbelief; but was strong in faith, giving glory to God; and being fully persuaded that, what he had promised, he was able also to perform" (Romans 4:20–21). He believed that the promise would be fulfilled, even though he and his wife were past the child-bearing years. Abraham was able

Two Worlds

to tap into the principles of the new world where age wasn't a factor! Faith transported his mind into the world where his biological condition wasn't a hindrance to what God had said. How was he going to have a child when he was old and his wife was old and barren? Everything of this world said it couldn't be done, and indeed by the laws of nature it shouldn't have happened, but Abraham's mindset defied the laws of nature.

You may not see what God is doing, but He's working in the background in the unseen world. All you have to do is give it to Him, believe in His Word, and He will make it happen. There's no lack or shortcomings in the Kingdom of God. It will be *"pressed down, and shaken together, and running over"* (Luke 6:38). All you have to do is receive the overflow.

If we can wrap our minds around the fact that the things we see and experience in this physical world don't have the final say over our situation, we will be able to experience the benefits of the spiritual world. How else can a woman say "It is well," knowing that her son is dead, unless she peeked into the Kingdom of God where death has no power? (2 Kings 4:8–37) How can a man enter into battle with only three hundred soldiers and come out victorious without shooting an arrow unless he put aside his human understanding and trusted the leader of the other world? (Judges 7).

How could an army go into war sending the worshippers first? Common sense says that you would be defeated unless you put your best men on the frontline, those who can withstand the harshness of battle. Yet God told the Israelites not to go to battle with the usual weapons, but instead to go with instruments, songs, and praises. How do you beat an army with timbrels when they have swords? Dare I say, Israel defeated this great army by slipping into the Kingdom of God and ignoring the earthly principles of war.

At times we are defeated because we refuse to believe in the process of the other world. We are so accustomed to doing it our way that we miss out on the Kingdom way. What God whispers in our spirit challenges what we know. If we try to use our humanity to understand the functions and rules that govern the spiritual world, we will forever be limited in the physical realm. We would never know that the lunch of a little boy could turn into an all-you-can-eat buffet. We must learn the rules that govern the new world in order to reap the benefits of living in two worlds.

THINK LIKE GOD

Jesus said, *"My kingdom is not of this world"* (John 18:36). If I choose to live in the Kingdom of God, I have to give up the world's system. In John 15:19, Jesus made it clear that we are not of the world because He has chosen us out of the world. He made a similar statement in John 17:16: *"They are not of the world, even as I am not of this world."*

Some could argue that since Jesus was not from here, it was much easier for Him to live by the Kingdom system. How can someone struggle with the Kingdom system when they don't know anything else? But remember, Jesus was born in Bethlehem, under the world's system. His parents, however, raised him up under God's system. This is proof that even though we were born and raised under the world's system, we are more than capable through Jesus Christ to transcend the dictates of our environment. Although we are trained and educated in the exploits of the kingdom of this world, Jesus has come into our lives to take up residency and shift us from one kingdom to another. This is the good work He has already begun in us, as mentioned in Philippians 1:6. This shift has to take place in our minds.

While we have to wait for things to happen in the physical world, it's true that everything is already done in the spiritual world. There are no unaccomplished, unfinished things in that realm. Jesus made a bold statement on the cross. He said, *"It is finished"* (John 19:30). Everything for our salvation, redemption, and wellbeing was accomplished on the cross. He was the Lamb slain before the foundation of the world (Revelation 13:8). That's why Jesus came to do the will of God. Everything Jesus did when He came to the earth was to demonstrate what God had already accomplished in the eternal. The Bible promises an increase in knowledge that will help us discover some hidden things that God has already done.

The challenge remains: how do we, who are wired to think practically and logically, operate in the other world? Can we flip from one world to another? Yes, we can! It is possible, once we understand that our possibilities in God aren't limited by our finiteness. As humans, we have limits and boundaries and can only do so much. Our understandings and capabilities are restricted. Even the greatest minds and inventors could only function by what was available to them. But in God, there are no restrictions, boundaries, or limitations.

Two Worlds

We can go where He goes and do what He does. Paul was caught up in the third heaven, and John was in the spirit on the Lord's Day when he saw the glorious One sitting on His throne. He was able to go into the future, but the operative word is "spirit." It is obvious from Paul's and John's experiences that you can be transported into another world, even into the future, while you remain in the physical realm. Phillip, the evangelist, was transported by the spirit after meeting and ministering to the Ethiopian eunuch (Acts 8:39). None of these men were angels or heavenly beings; they were humans, just like us, yet they were able to gain great insight into the other world.

How do we become a part of this new world? First, we must believe. None of what God says will happen in our lives until we first know that these things are in His Word and that He wants us to experience them here on earth. We can experience them if we believe that everything God has said is possible.

Faith isn't one of the components of the mind, but it does affect the mind on another level. Faith is what I call the sixth sense. It's the only link between man and God, between the natural and the supernatural, between the physical and the spiritual, the kingdom of man and the Kingdom of God.

The Bible says, *"Now faith is the substance of things hoped for, the evidence of things not seen"* (Hebrews 11:1). That statement is almost an oxymoron, as it appears to contradict itself. How can something that cannot be seen be evidence? In this world, that doesn't make sense. If a lawyer attempts to defend a client with evidence that cannot be seen, or a witness who doesn't exist, he would definitely lose the case. In this world, evidence must be tangible to be effective, but in the Kingdom of God our faith brings what cannot be seen into the seen and makes the intangible tangible.

Paul said, *"While we look not at the things which are seen, but at the things which are not seen: for the things which are seen are temporal; but the things which are not seen are eternal"* (2 Corinthians 4:18). The more we extend our faith and think on the things not seen, the more we will believe in the principles of the new world, the more our thought processes will change, and the more we will begin to think like God.

chapter seven
TRANSFORMING THE MIND

WHY DO I STILL THINK LIKE A MAN WHEN THE BIBLE STATES THAT I HAVE THE mind of Christ? (1 Corinthians 2:16) Could it be that my mind hasn't been transformed? The word *transform* means for us to be changed or to have a new way of thinking. So if my mind has been transformed, there should be a dramatic change to my thought process. I can no longer think in the same manner, and therefore I cannot process information, situations, and circumstances the way I used to. I will no longer see things through the eyes of my experiences, education, or biases. It will be the God-way of thinking.

Paul warns us in Romans 12:2 that we should not be *"conformed to this world: but be ye transformed by the renewing of your mind."* There's no way we can take on the image of God if we look like the world, and we cannot think like God if our thoughts are wrapped up in the logic of the world. To experience this great transformation, our minds must be converted, or spiritually awakened. Our minds must be restored to a state which reflects the image of God.

Something cannot be renewed unless the old layers are stripped away. We must separate ourselves from the worldly way of thinking. There has to be a synchronizing of our minds with the mind of God. This transformation process is important if we are going to 1) know the thoughts of God and 2) have the thoughts of God. If this change doesn't take place, nothing God downloads into us will have any value or effect. God's plan for us won't become a reality if we only see things through a worldly view. We must make a conscious effort to release our old thoughts and allow the thoughts of God to penetrate our minds.

This is a battle for our thoughts. Not only do we have to fight the basic thoughts we've learned over our lifespan, but we must also fight the thoughts of the devil that are trying to inundate our minds to go against the will of God. The only way to win this battle and have our minds transformed is to use the weapon that Paul describes this way:

> *For the weapons of our warfare are not carnal, but mighty through God to the pulling down of strong holds... casting down* imaginations, *and every high thing that exalteth itself against the knowledge of God, and bringing into captivity every* thought *to the obedience of Christ.*
> —2 Corinthians 10:4–5 (emphasis added)

We must be cognizant of the thoughts we entertain. Are they evil, vain, or rebellious? Do they oppose the principles of the Word of God? If so, Paul said we must cast down or destroy them and bring them into captivity. When someone is held captive, they have no authority or power over their captors. They are not in control of the situation. Similarly, when we bring our thoughts into captivity, they will no longer have authority or power over us. They are brought into obedience to the Word of God.

The renewing of one's mind has to be intentional and continuous. Every day I must reflect on the state of my mind and the thoughts it produces. Are my thoughts in alignment with God's Word? If they aren't in alignment, I won't become a God-thinker. If I'm not a God-thinker, my actions will not be of God. For example, if I'm presented with an attractive business offer—maybe it would yield a nice profit but isn't one hundred percent legitimate—my carnal mind would instruct me to sign the deal. But my renewed mind wouldn't entertain the offer, since the Word of God speaks against dishonesty. Once I've brought my thoughts into captivity, my carnal mind has no control over my spiritual mind. What I have done in this case is exchange my thoughts for His thoughts, my human way of thinking for the God-way of thinking.

Meditation

Meditating on the Word of God is the key to renewing your mind and becoming a God-thinker. Generally speaking, meditation is a technique used to relax the mind by changing one's focus from the external to the internal.

Meditating on the Word calls for a designated time when you are alone somewhere quiet, not thinking about the world around you or the situations you're currently experiencing; your focus is on the Word, its meaning, and how God intends to use it to impact your life.

It's difficult at first to still the mind and drown out the external world, but with time this becomes easier. Eventually your thought process will be impacted by the Word, which will then impact your words and actions. Jesus said, *"[T]he words that I speak unto you, they are spirit, and they are life"* (John 6:63). God's Word is not of the flesh but of the spirit. It nourishes the soul and gives life to those who need to be revived and restored. Therefore, if I can digest His Word and train my mind to meditate on it, I will begin to speak things into being.

Regardless of the situation, we must think spirit and we must think life if we are to think like God. The same Spirit that moved upon the face of the deep and made order and beauty out of nothing can do the same in our lives if we just think like God. We have become sub-humans when we're supposed to be superhuman. If you think about it, superheroes have nothing on us!

The Benefits of Meditation

Many scriptures state the benefits of meditating on the Word of God, such as Isaiah 26:3: *"Thou wilt keep him in perfect peace, whose mind is stayed on thee: because he trusteth in thee."* Peace is the missing ingredient in this world of war, sickness, and death. But it is obtainable to those whose minds are focused on God. Isaiah describes this type of peace as "perfect," which simply means that it is divine; it is of God. Therefore, it cannot be impacted by poverty, financial distress, health issues, or any other of life's storms. If you have the peace of God reigning in your soul and mind, you won't go through these experiences. The storms of life will no longer dictate how you behave, the decisions you make, or the words you speak.

> *But his delight is in the law of the Lord; and in his law doth he meditate day and night. And he shall be like a tree planted by the rivers of water, that bringeth*

Transforming the Mind

forth his fruit in his season; his leaf also shall not wither; and whatsoever he doeth shall prosper.

—Psalm 1:2–3

Notice that the psalmist finds "delight" in the law of the Lord. It is a pleasure and a joy for him to study the commandments and truth of the Word. This excitement for the Word propelled him to meditate.

The result of meditating on Scripture is outlined where the psalmist compares the individual who meditates to a tree planted by a river. This is not a wild tree whose seeds are blown by the wind and take root wherever they fall. This tree has been carefully planted, cultivated, and strategically placed by a river. "[D]ivisions of water [is a] term used in the East for small channels which divide a garden for purposes of irrigation."[2] Because of the proper irrigation, this tree was fruitful and flourishing. The leaves of this tree, was green and lush. Fruit "symbolizes increase or multiplication" and leaf symbolizes "life amidst prosperity or adversity.[3] This is in direct relation to Galatians 5:22–23, which speaks of the fruit of the Spirit—love, joy, peace, long-suffering, gentleness, goodness, faith, meekness, and temperance. Meditation on Scripture will yield the fruit of the Spirit in your life.

The psalmist continues to say that whatever a meditator does, it will prosper. Imagine that everything you do, whether spiritual or natural, prospers. Imagine that every investment you make yields a great return. It is possible if you're a God-thinker.

Unfortunately, in today's society our delight is not in the Bible, but in magazines, television programs, music, and other forms of entertainment. We make sure we record a movie or basketball game if we're unable to watch it at the designated time, allowing us to view it later that day or week. We take time out of our busy schedules to plan social events or hang out with friends. There's nothing wrong with these types of activities or social events, but if you want to be a God-thinker it is imperative to have balance. God must be part of your daily schedule. The Bible says we should exercise ourselves in

---

2 Finis Jennings Dake, *The Dake Annotated Reference Bible, KJV* (Lawrenceville, GA: Dake Publishing, 1991), 549.

3 Kevin J. Conner, *Interpreting the Symbols and Types* (Portland, OR: Bible Temple Publishing, 1992), 145, 152.

godliness. If we want to experience the benefits of meditation, we have to do it over and over again. As the old saying goes, practice makes perfect.

We have to train our minds. I encourage you to pinpoint something you want to see happen in your life or ministry. Find the scripture that's relevant to your situation and begin to think on it. The law of attraction "is the ability to attract into our lives whatever we are focusing on."[4] By focusing on positive or negative thoughts, you can bring positive or negative experiences into your life. If you're thinking of buying a Mercedes Benz but haven't bought it yet, notice that from the day it was conceived in your mind every other car you see is a Benz. If this happens when we think on natural things, can you imagine what would happen if we should begin to think on spiritual things? It is said that we are what we think: *"For as he thinketh in his heart, so is he"* (Proverbs 23:7). This is why the Bible explicitly encourages us,

> *Finally, brethren, whatsoever things are true, whatsoever things are honest, whatsoever things are just, whatsoever things are pure, whatsoever things are lovely, whatsoever things are of good report; if there be any virtue, and if there be any praise, think on these things.*
>
> —Philippians 4:8

Begin to think on God's Word and you will begin to experience His bliss, His power, and your rightful position in the earthly realm. You will be able to do godly things. God is about to take you places you've never been before. Every God-thinker experiences abundant life; every God-thinker is a winner! Your life is about to change.

I like to do the following mental exercise to prove the power of meditation. If you close your eyes and think about a lemon, your mouth will begin to salivate. You will feel the same sensation as if you were actually eating a lemon. Try it for yourself. The nature of the lemon is sour. Meditating on the lemon alone, without actually eating it, produces the taste or nature of the lemon in your mouth.

---

4   The Law of Attraction, "What Is the Law of Attraction? Open Your Eyes to a World of Endless Possibilities." Date of access: December 6, 2017 (http://www.thelawofattraction.com/what-is-the-law-of-attraction/).

Transforming the Mind

The nature of the Word is life and spirit. Everything God is exists in His Word. Meditating on the Word will bring into our lives the very nature or content of the Word. For example, if you want to be healed, what do you think will happen if you start thinking about being healed? In the same way that thinking about a lemon produces a sour taste in our mouths, meditating on the healing words of the Bible brings to us every healing virtue that is in our Lord Jesus.

Joshua was told that if he meditated on the Word day and night, he would *"have good success"* (Joshua 1:8). I guarantee that no matter how long you've been going through your situation, you have the power to change it. Be still and wrap your mind around the Word of God.

chapter eight
Transition into the Kingdom of God

Paul wrote to the Colossians, "Who hath delivered us from the power of darkness, and hath translated us into the kingdom of his dear Son" (Colossians 1:13).

One of the definitions of the word *translate* is "to remove from one place to another" or "to turn from one language to another."[5] This can be likened to the life cycle of a butterfly, which consists of four stages. The first stage begins with the adult female butterfly laying eggs. The second stage is the caterpillar, the third stage is the chrysalis, and the last stage is the butterfly. To become a butterfly, the caterpillar needs to move into the chrysalis stage. However, if it remains in the chrysalis stage it will never become a butterfly.

Many Christians seem to get trapped in the chrysalis stage. They begin the process but find it difficult to immerse themselves in the Kingdom lifestyle. They're faithful in their service to the Lord and the church. However, they must realize that attending church regularly, and singing on the praise and worship team, doesn't mean that they have successfully made the shift to the Kingdom lifestyle. There are many people who are faithful to their duties in the church but still live their lives based on the world system.

Paul told the Corinthian church that it was impossible for him to address them as people who live in the spirit. He had to address them as though they were living in the world because they hadn't matured in the spirit; they still acted like children. He said, *"I have fed you with milk, and not with meat: for hitherto ye were not able to bear it, neither yet now are ye able"* (1 Corinthians 3:2). Is it possible to be faithful and still struggle to make the transition? Jesus said,

---

5 *Online Etymology Dictionary*, "Translate." Date of access: December 21, 2017 (https://www.etymonline.com/word/translate).

Transition into the Kingdom of God

Not every one that saith unto me, Lord, Lord, shall enter into the kingdom of heaven; but he that doeth the will of my Father which is in heaven. Many will say to me in that day, Lord, Lord, have we not prophesied in thy name? and in thy name have cast out devils? and in thy name done many wonderful works? And then will I profess unto them, I never knew you: depart from me, ye that work iniquity.

—Matthew 7:21–23

These were obviously believers who prophesied and did wonderful things in the name of Jesus. It speaks to the fact that the manifestation of the gifts doesn't mean that the transition has been made. I can operate in my gifts and still be a carnal Christian, because what I do is based on the system of the world. I have to make a lifestyle change to make the transition into the Kingdom. It's not something I do on a Sunday morning, but a choice I make to live my life based upon the Word of God, regardless of my circumstances.

Paul wrote to the Romans, *"Do not conform to the pattern of this world, but be transformed by the renewing of your mind. Then you will be able to test and approve what God's will is—his good, pleasing and perfect will"* (Romans 12:2, NIV). The transformation has to take place in the mind.

Do you see why people can spend years in the church, being faithful to the duties of the church, and not experience Kingdom bliss?

I will never forget the words of the master of ceremonies at a graduation I attended. He said, "The illiterate of the twenty-first century aren't the people who can't read, but the people who are learned but don't have the ability to unlearn and relearn." Nobody progresses into the Kingdom without relearning. I understand the difficulties of learning the things of a different Kingdom. It isn't easy to unlearn or dismantle our established mindset. Every day is a battle to understand God and His ways. If He were a man, we would be able to analyze Him and make our determination. The challenge is this: that which is mortal must comprehend the immortal, and that which is finite must comprehend that which is infinite.

Let us consider for a moment one of the laws of His Kingdom: *"Love your enemies, bless them that curse you, do good to them that hate you, and pray for them which despitefully use you, and persecute you"* (Matthew 5:44). Our finite minds don't want us to love our enemies, and they definitely don't want us to do good to them. How can we do good to someone who's trying to assassinate our character? Our natural reaction is to do to them what they have done to us—an eye for an eye and a tooth for a tooth.

However, we must remember that we have been translated into the Kingdom of His dear Son, and if we want to prosper and have good success we have no choice but to unlearn our vengeful ways and subject ourselves to the ways of the Kingdom. The Kingdom instruction for this situation states that vengeance belongs to God and He will repay it. It teaches us to forgive those who trespass against us. Matthew 6:14 states, *"For if ye forgive men their trespasses, your heavenly Father will also forgive you."* In essence, if our minds aren't transformed, regardless of how long we spend in the church, we won't be ready to handle the things of the Kingdom, much less be elevated to the next level in God.

Jesus says in Mathew 11:29, *"Take my yoke upon you, and* learn of me; for I am meek and lowly in heart: and ye shall find rest unto your souls" (emphasis added). This is an actual invitation to take Kingdom classes. We are invited to learn the ways of the King. The Bible also says that *"his ways [are] past finding out"* (Romans 11:33). Therefore, He is the only one who can teach us His ways. It is for this reason that man doesn't know God by his own wisdom; he can only know God by way of revelation. He is unorthodox and illogical in His ways.

God doesn't always work from a logical position. He defies the reasoning of man. Scientists cannot research Him. He cannot be discovered. He is God and only He can uncover himself. When God uncovers Himself to us, we must be willing to unlearn everything we were taught in the kingdom of the world and intoxicate our minds with His knowledge. The great Apostle Paul wrote,

> *Yea doubtless, and I count all things but loss for the excellency of the knowledge of Christ Jesus my Lord: for whom I have suffered the loss of all things, and do count them but dung, that I may win Christ... that I may know him, and the power of his resurrection, and the fellowship of his sufferings, being made conformable unto his death.*
>
> —Philippians 3:8, 10

It is obvious that Paul had to go through a serious mind adjustment. He had to devalue what he knew for the excellency of His knowledge. In other words, he had to unlearn and relearn. I'm convinced that ninety percent of

Transition into the Kingdom of God

the bondage people bear isn't demonic. It's mental. It isn't easy to disregard everything you know and learn something that at times doesn't make sense to the cognitive functions of man.

I believe that the greatest threat to the church today isn't the devil. It can't be the devil, for we are told in Scripture that the devil is a liar and that the gates of hell shall not prevail against the church. When we resist him, he will flee. So what is the problem? Sometimes we're held back by what we know. The Bible says that Jesus, who was God manifested in the flesh, *"did not many mighty works there because of [the people's] unbelief"* (Matthew 13:58). Imagine, God couldn't demonstrate His power and do much among them because of their mindset. Their minds were focused on what they knew about Him. They knew He was a carpenter's son; they knew His mother's name; they knew that His brothers and sisters lived in the same neighborhood as they did. In other words, how could Jesus work miracles when His family were regular people who lived amongst us? The Bible says they were offended at Him.

When God reveals new things, we are often required to let go of the old things and move in the spirit of His progressive revelation. We cannot at any cost allow the culture or traditions of men to cause us to miss out on the bliss of the Kingdom. The Old Testament scriptures explicitly describe God's evidential presence among His people. The evidence that He dwells among His people was irrefutable and undeniable.

God wants to do the same for us in this generation, but we cannot shut him up in a cultural or a denominational box and expect Kingdom bliss. The God of Abraham and Isaac transcends the dictates of our environment, denomination, and finiteness. The Bible says, *"There is no speech nor language, where [His] voice is not heard"* (Psalm 19:3). God must be heard in every square foot of planet Earth. He must be heard in the first, second, and third heavens. He must be heard beyond our concept of who we think He is.

I have often heard the saying, "Take the limits off God." However, I don't agree with it. God has no limits or boundaries; the limits are in us. The mindset of Kingdom people should be *"but with God all things are possible"* (Matthew 19:26) and that nothing is too hard for the Lord to do (Jeremiah 32:27). God is getting ready to shock the world, so we must be ready to grasp Him and move with Him as He reveals more of Himself to us. He is about to bring us from the back to the front, from obscurity to prominence.

Think Like God

We are now in God's set time. Therefore, we must position ourselves in Him so He can show the world who He is and who we are in Him. He is about to do things that our forefathers have neither seen nor heard of. God is getting ready to move beyond our church walls. He is in the streets, raising up a new breed of reject, moving them into position to be major soul-winners in these last days. The day of normal is over. I see in the very near future the explosion of the Kingdom of God upon the earth. Unfortunately, He won't be using "normal church people" to do it, because in God's set time He cannot use people who are set in their religious ways.

I once heard the Lord say, "It is a radical move that needs radical-minded people. I will call for the extremist and the impure and I will garner their spirits and change their focus for this last push on the earth. I will use the uncertified to certify my positon, the unqualified to qualify my people for the rapture. I am God and I shall bring this thing to pass in your days. I shall marvel the religious order, because the men and women, the boys and girls, I shall use in my set time is of no set order; they shall do as I command and they shall go where I send them, for they are mine. Many shall marvel at me, but my works and my hands will be seen and then they shall know that I, God, am no respecter of persons."

How do we make this transition? It is necessary for us to commit ourselves totally to the Word of God. The Word is the very expression of God's mind guiding us into the ways and mindset of the King. John wrote, *"In the beginning was the Word, and the Word was with God, and the Word was God"* (John 1:1). Jesus said in John 5:39 that the scriptures testify of Him. If I want to know God, I have no other way of knowing Him but by reading His Word.

As previously mentioned, His Kingdom is not from here. Therefore, we must go to the source which tells us about Him and how we ought to conduct ourselves in this Kingdom. For this reason, when we approach Scripture we must surrender everything we know and allow the Word to tell us who this King is and what His Kingdom is like.

I love to tell this story. When I was about fourteen years old, I had a class assignment to read a book and write an essay. I wrote the essay, which included a large amount of research from the Oxford English Dictionary. Of course, I felt a sense of accomplishment. I waited impatiently for my mark with pride.

Transition into the Kingdom of God

When I received the essay from my teacher, I felt as if I had been hit by a thunderbolt! I saw two red marks on each corner of my paper, and they looked like an X. My disappointment was beyond expression. I could hardly wait to find out what I had done to be so rewarded.

Finally, I was able to speak to the teacher. The words that came out of her mouth have remained with me to this day.

"Richard, you did great," she said. "Your presentation was lovely and your words were used in the right context." This only mystified me further. If I had done so well, what was the problem? Then she gave it to me: "You didn't capture the mind of the writer, even though your presentation was lovely."

Sometimes we prepare beautiful presentations from the Word of God and we feel as though we have received the revelation of our lifetime. However, if the revelation or presentation doesn't reflect the mind of God, we've just wasted our time. In addition, we have jeopardized the faith of God's people, because they will place their faith in man's philosophy.

The harsh reality is that if something you hear isn't the mind of God, no matter how good it sounds, it's man's philosophy. Many people in the body of Christ are going through what I call "God hurt." They've put their faith in someone's philosophy and thought they were receiving a word from God, only to find out years later that they invested their faith in man's philosophy and didn't receive the result they were expecting. Therefore, they blame God.

It's impossible to put one's faith in the Word of God and not see results. God said in Isaiah 55:11, "So shall my word be that goeth forth out of my mouth: it shall not return unto me void, but it shall accomplish that which I please, and it shall prosper in the thing whereto I sent it."

In Paul's presentation to the Corinthians, he was careful not to use enticing words of man's wisdom but the demonstration of the spirit and power to ensure that their faith wouldn't stand in the wisdom of men but in the power of God (I Corinthians 2:4).

Faith in man's wisdom cannot move God; it doesn't give us access to Kingdom possibilities. I wonder how many times God has written an "X" on our paper and we cannot see it. Our presentation may sound good and it resonates with people, so we hold onto it and make a doctrine out of something that's not the expression of the mind of God. It becomes popular with the masses, and we continue to feed them with it for our own gain and fame. The

Think Like God

Bible says in Jeremiah 23:1, *"Woe be unto the pastors that destroy and scatter the sheep of my pasture!"* We who have been given the ability to impart the Word must be diligent when it comes to feeding the flock.

In Deuteronomy 4:2, we read, *"Ye shall not add unto the word which I command you, neither shall ye diminish ought from it, that ye may keep the commandments of the Lord your God which I command you."* Genesis shows us how destructive adding or taking away from God's Word can be. Satan took away and added, and the result is seen in the world today. The whole creation is currently in a dilemma. Man is on a downward spiral, moving from one extreme of sin and wickedness to another. Satan knew that the only way to conquer mankind and the world was to feed him something God forbade him to eat.

As I said before, we must be very careful what we feed God's people. One of the greatest attacks against the church isn't coming from the world, but rather from men and women who preach and teach erroneous doctrines to the people of God. Unfortunately, some of us don't care what we eat as long as we're being fed something.

The misinterpretation of Scripture, no matter how good it sounds, won't transition you into His Kingdom. I realize that I have to be diligent when I apply the Word of God to receive the results I need. The Word has to be applied precisely, as God commanded.

Let us consider King Saul's narrative. God told him to slay all the Amalekites. Did he slay the Amalekites? Yes, he did, but God said to slay *all*. I probably would have given him a pass, or simply rewarded him for obeying part of the instruction. However, in God's sight, Saul totally disobeyed His Word and so He rejected him. This speaks to the fact that God cannot reward us for a half-hearted application of His Word. He told the people in Deuteronomy 28:1–2,

> *And it shall come to pass, if thou shalt hearken diligently unto the voice of the Lord thy God, to observe and to do all his commandments which I command thee this day, that the Lord thy God will set thee on high above all nations of the earth: and all these blessings shall come on thee, and overtake thee, if thou shalt hearken unto the voice of the Lord thy God.*

Transition into the Kingdom of God

Success in the world or in the Kingdom of God doesn't happen by chance; we have to be precise, diligent, and observant. When we think we're obeying His Word and don't receive the desired results, our level of frustration is hard to express. Many times, I have to go to God in prayer and ask Him, "What am I doing wrong?"

God can see the difference between words and actions; there are times when my actions don't endorse my words or my words don't endorse my actions. I have to bring my words and actions under the submission of His Word. Doing good to my enemies isn't just something I ought to say. My actions can't say, "I'm just doing this because the Bible says I should" or "If I had my way, I wouldn't even give them a slice of bread." Our actions often aren't in alignment with our words.

The truth is, to receive the desired results out of the Word of God, we sometimes have to do it until it hurts. The Apostle James says, *"But be ye doers of the word, and not hearers only, deceiving your own selves"* (James 1:22). Repetition is the art of perfection. We can't be like the man who was so tired of praying to God every night that he wrote his prayer on a piece of paper and hung it on the wall. Every night before he went to bed, he would look at his prayer on the wall and say, "Same thing again, God." We must be prepared to do the same thing again and again until we experience a breakthrough. We cannot get tired of doing it.

The Bible says that we must *"not be weary in well doing"* (Galatians 6:9). It also gives an account of the widow who repeatedly went to a judge with a request. Scripture says that the judge feared neither God nor man, but the widow continued to make her request until she received what she wanted. In other words, transitioning into the Kingdom is going to take repetition. If you and I aren't prepared to do that, we will never see the mighty hand of God moving in our lives.

We must remember that God blesses faithfulness, and everything about God is governed by time and place. Ecclesiastes 3:1 says, *"To every thing there is a season."* That's why we have to keep doing what God has said until the fullness of time has come in our lives.

It's obvious from Paul's statement regarding carnal Christians that long-standing church membership doesn't transition one into the Kingdom of God. It's the transformation of the mind. It's the ability to understand

Kingdom principles and living. Kingdom principles and living usually go against our human tendencies. It can become frustrating, discouraging, and disappointing to follow the requirements of the Kingdom. It's much easier to fulfill the desires of the flesh.

Paul says, *"But I keep under my body, and bring it into subjection: lest that by any means, when I have preached to others, I myself should be a castaway"* (1 Corinthians 9:27). It's great to preach Kingdom principles, but we have to ensure that we see the fruits of our messages in our lives. When Paul said that he bore the mark of Christ in his body (Galatians 6:17), he was referring to the pains that resulted from him being constantly submitted to the will of God. It is this constant inward battle that causes many people not to strive for excellence; instead they settle for mediocrity.

Many sit in the pew or stand behind the pulpit on a Sunday morning, but they've given up and don't have the passion to strive for masteries—to strive to be superior, a passion to be better—because every time they put their heart into the work of the Lord they get hurt. It doesn't help that many preachers remove the cross from their messages. Jesus said, *"If any man will come after me, let him deny himself, and take up his cross, and follow me"* (Matthew 16:24). I wish all the successful men and women of God who have gone through the grinding and winding journey would speak more about it. We are often misled by these people's achievements because we have no knowledge of the journey. There's always a story behind the glory, and the subject of their stories is pain.

God told Abraham that his seed would sojourn into a strange land and there be multiplied. Genesis 22:17 says,

> *That in blessing I will bless thee, and in multiplying I will multiply thy seed as the stars of the heaven, and as the sand which is upon the sea shore; and thy seed shall possess the gate of his enemies.*

The Bible says that seventy of his descendants went down to Egypt. However, when God was ready to fulfill His Word to Abraham, to multiply them, He did it through the oppression of the Egyptians. Scripture clearly states that the more Abraham's people were afflicted by the Egyptians, the

Transition into the Kingdom of God

more they increased and multiplied. Affliction wasn't designed to destroy them but to increase them.

Let us look at Samson, who was anointed by God. However, the anointing only came upon him when he faced opposition. Every time Delilah said, "Samson, Samson, the Philistines are upon you," the Spirit of God came upon him. We weren't made to die under pressure. Quite the contrary. Pressure and affliction causes increase and multiplication in the lives of Kingdom people.

I'm not suggesting that we should look for trouble, but we must not dismiss the events of the cross, for the cross helps us in the transitional process. The Bible says, *"But as it is written, Eye hath not seen, nor ear heard, neither have entered into the heart of man, the things which God hath prepared for them that love him"* (1 Corinthians 2:9). If God were to release His blessings in our lives without the cross experience, we wouldn't be able to handle it. God wants to ensure that when He takes us to the pinnacle of His blessings, we will be able to stay there. It brings no glory or praise to Him if we can't remain in His place of blessings.

Many have tried to reach this pinnacle other ways but were destroyed by pride. The Apostle Peter says, *"Forasmuch then as Christ hath suffered for us in the flesh, arm yourselves likewise with the same mind: for he that hath suffered in the flesh hath ceased from sin"* (1 Peter 4:1) In Psalm 119:71, David said that he was glad when he was afflicted.

I'm a living testimony. I've been through some very dark periods in my journey with God. I have noticed that anytime God is going to take me to another level, I have to pass through a storm, and I have to conquer the enemy before God moves me forward.

The situations you're experiencing right now are preparing you for Kingdom advancement. God is preparing you for something bigger than your dreams. In Joseph's dreams, his brothers and father bowed before him. After the dark experiences, God took him to places that were bigger than his dreams. Not only did his brothers and father bow to him, but he was a prominent ruler in the land of Egypt.

The cross helps us to come to the end of ourselves. God cannot and will not advance us in the Kingdom until we come to the place of acknowledging that it's not by might or by strength but one hundred percent by the spirit of God.

THINK LIKE GOD

As we saw in Joseph's life, there is no straight path to one's destiny. Before the pilot gets into the cockpit, he knows where he's going and the destination is fixed, but the path oftentimes takes the plane in another direction to get to its destination. God has a chartered path for each of us. We often get discouraged because where we are on the journey seemingly has nothing to do with where we want to go, or where God has said He's going to take us. Many of us abort our own journeys because we don't understand the process God uses to prepare us for something greater.

Joseph went from the prison life to the throne life. His prison experience certainly wasn't indicative of where he was going. However, according to God's divine plan, it was necessary for him to make a pit stop in prison.

Where you are now in your journey with God isn't permanent. It's just a pit stop.

We haven't learned well the lesson to put the Kingdom first. That's why we aren't where we think we should be in God. The dreams and visions we receive are from God, but they won't materialize until we learn this most valuable Kingdom lesson—put the Kingdom first. Matthew 6:33 states, *"But seek ye first the kingdom of God, and his righteousness; and all these things shall be added unto you."* He will add blessings to our lives if we seek Him first. Serving in the Kingdom selflessly is a lesson many of us struggle with.

I recently went on a trip to St. Vincent and Grenada for a revival service. I had to fly from Trinidad to Grenada, then to St. Vincent. On my way to Grenada, God asked me a few questions.

"Are you doing this for self-upliftment or for the love of the gospel?" He asked. "If you had a church with thousands of members and I sent you to one of the most remote parts of the world to save someone, would you leave your church to go to this remote place for this one soul?"

Before this experience, I had been struggling with God regarding my personal life. I had been asking God, "What's in it for me?" I felt that I was working hard in the Kingdom of God, but my personal desires weren't being met. I almost decided not to move another muscle until I knew what was in it for me.

God waited until I was on a plane to speak to me. The questions God asked compelled me to search deep into my soul. As I searched, I literally felt emotional pain. It wasn't until I was sharing my experience with a friend that the answers came to me. The reason I was traveling to Grenada was due to the love I had for the gospel of Jesus Christ. There were no earthly rewards for me to gain, but I would receive a few heavenly crowns for the seven people I had baptized in the name of Jesus. Before this trip, I had set some goals that I wanted to achieve in my ministry; I still want to achieve them today, but if God doesn't lead me, I have a deep and sincere conviction not to seek them.

This confrontation with God caused me to give Him my ambitions and take His will. No one will be successful in kingdom living if they can't learn this basic lesson. It's not about us. It's about God. If we can't get past ourselves, we will never get to God.

I find it much easier to get past people, but very difficult to get pass myself. We attend seminars and study hard to be masters of others, because we believe that mastering others will make us more successful. This approach, of course, won't make us better leaders. As a matter of fact, I think it only qualifies us to be good church manipulators, not godly leaders. My friends, I have learned that it is the mastering of myself that brings glory to God, positioning me to seek His Kingdom first.

Another valuable lesson I learned on that trip is that some of our assignments from God aren't about results, but about obedience. God was never in agreement with child sacrifice, but He told Abraham to sacrifice his only son, Isaac. Was God agreeing to child sacrifice in that case? Of course not! Before God established Abraham any further, He had to know where his heart was. Was he willing to obey Him in just some things, or in all things? What is in our lives that God can't have? Abraham displayed total commitment to God. God was first in his life, insomuch that he was willing to give up his only son for God.

Sometimes God withholds His blessings from us because there's something or someone standing between us and God. That thing or person is taking God's place in our lives. It could be as simple as a desire we have. It's not that God doesn't want us to have some of these things or persons in our lives; He just wants them to be in the right priority. He must be first. The Bible says that He *"might have the preeminence"* (Colossians 1:18).

The beautiful thing about the Kingdom first philosophy is that whatever we may lose in the process, God has said that He will add these things unto us, that He will provide for our needs. God is looking for someone to trust with His blessings. He found Abraham, who, although he became rich, remained constant in his relationship and faith towards God. God is seeking someone who will ensure that He is first in their life, regardless of their earthly possessions. God doesn't release blessings in the lives of people who are going to eventually replace Him or make Him second in their lives. If He was first when we had nothing, He must remain first after He has blessed us.

David, a man after God's own heart, was able to slay Goliath, but he couldn't slay the desires of his flesh. He took another's man's wife and committed murder to hide the destruction of his behavior. How many giants have we slain? Some of us have slain all our giants except for one: the one in the mirror. If the giant in the mirror is still standing tall and strong in your life, your chances of succeeding in the Kingdom of God are low.

I must define and see myself the way God defines and sees me. If we don't learn that lesson, we'll stay in the Kingdom of God and long for the endorsement and confirmation of the kingdom of the world. Numbers 13:33 states, *"And there we saw the giants, the sons of Anak, which come of the giants: and we were in our own sight as grasshoppers, and so we were in their sight."* The Israelites saw themselves as grasshoppers, and it's noticeable that their enemies saw the Israelites the same way—as grasshoppers. Our enemies are going to see us the same way we see ourselves. More importantly, we will become that which we see ourselves. The enemy didn't have to fight the Israelites to win; they defeated themselves the moment they saw themselves as grasshoppers. If we keep portraying ourselves as weaklings, the devil will defeat us. We must portray strength even in our weakest moments, as stated in 2 Corinthians 12:10: *"for when I am weak, then am I strong."*

My value and purpose are no longer defined by the ways of the world. In the world, if you have a little money in the bank people call you "sir," but in God's kingdom you can be broke as ever and still called "son." What do I want to be called? Sir or son? I don't know about you, but I want the King of Kings and Lord of Lords to call me son. I am everything that God said I am. I am not defined by my circumstances or by the people around me. I will not give any man the power to belittle me with their definitions. The devil needs to know he isn't contending with grasshoppers, but rather with the sons of God. The same way our circumstance cannot change our DNA, we are who

Transition into the Kingdom of God

we are regardless of the vicissitudes of life. We must not allow our circumstances to change us from who God says we are.

Transitioning into the Kingdom of God is impossible without the Word of God, which is the mind of God. Satan doesn't want our earthly possessions; he wants our minds to be conformed to this world, and in so doing we will miss out on our true potential in God.

Look at the relationship God had with Adam before the fall. They would commune with each other in the cool of the day. How about Abraham? God wouldn't destroy Sodom and Gomorrah without telling him. Moses stood up before God and asked Him not to destroy the people, and God listened. Elijah shut up the rain in heaven for three and a half years.

We are called to represent God in holiness and in power. We must cease to exert our power and seek instead to position ourselves in God's Word so we can exert His power and be true representatives of Him. Paul said, *"And my speech and my preaching was not with enticing words of man's wisdom, but in demonstration of the Spirit and of power"* (1 Corinthians 2:4). It's time for us to take our place on the earth by taking our place in the Word.

Someone once told me that words are the mirror of the mind. Every Word of God mirrors His thoughts. When we align ourselves with His Word, we align ourselves with His thoughts, and when we align ourselves with His thoughts, we are in the position to take our place and represent Him. Take your place in the Word in order to take your place in the earth.

Satan cannot rob us of our place here on the earth if we keep the Word. Satan doesn't want us to stop going to church, or to leave the praise and worship team. What he wants is to marginalize and minimize us, to keep us beneath our divine potential so we won't experience our maximum power in God. I guarantee you that once we get a taste of God's maximum power, we won't be able to go back to minimum experiences.

The Bible says that we are workers together with Him (2 Corinthians 6:1). If the powers of darkness were defeated by God's power, why would He intentionally give us less power to do the same job? He would be setting us up to fail. If I'm working with Him, I must have the same power He has; I must be able to do the same things on the earth that He did. Jesus Himself said that we would do greater works than He (John 14:12), and therefore we need the power He operated in. Since God called me from the world of sin to operate like Him in the earthly realm, I should be able to do what He did when He was here in the flesh and make that transition into the Kingdom of God!

chapter nine
THINK LIKE GOD

I BELIEVE THAT MAN CAN THINK LIKE GOD, AND BY NOW YOU SHOULD ALSO realize that we are more than capable of possessing His mind. This must be the goal of every believer. The Bible itself tells us, *"Let this mind be in you, which was also in Christ Jesus"* (Philippians 2:5). God wouldn't have included this in His Word if it was impossible for us to attain.

While examining the capabilities of the human mind in Chapter One, we saw how great the mind of man can be. This was evident in the recount of the tower of Babel in Genesis 11:1–9. God had to confound the people because He saw that *"as one people speaking the same language, they have begun to do this, then nothing they plan to do will be impossible for them"* (Genesis 11:6, NIV). So if we set our minds on thinking like God, it can be accomplished.

No one was born a surgeon or scientist, but after years of training they see the world from the specialty in which they were trained. A doctor will often rush to the aid of someone choking even when he is off-duty. A fireman on vacation will run into a burning building to help rescue someone, almost instinctively, because this is what she or he was trained to do. It has become a part of them. This proves that the mind can be trained to think a certain way. If we train our minds in the ways of the Kingdom of God, we will think like Kingdom people.

Having accepted Jesus Christ as our Savior and chosen to follow Him, He *"delivered us from the power of darkness, and hath translated us into the kingdom of his dear Son"* (Colossians 1:13). Now that we are translated, we must learn to think like the King and adjust ourselves through the transforming of our minds to exist in His Kingdom.

Think Like God

Making the Switch

The reason many of us struggle to make the switch from man's way of thinking to God's way is that the devil has deceived us into believing that thinking and living in the worldly system is the only way. He has caused us to focus on the things that are seen more than the unseen—the things we can justify, understand, and rationally explain through our senses.

We have already reviewed the importance of identifying the thoughts of the devil. It may not be evil thoughts that lead us to hateful actions, but when we're confronted with real life issues like mortgage payments, illnesses, and other human concerns, we have to make the switch. Although these concerns are very real and the cares of life can become overwhelming, we cannot get caught up in them. That's what the devil wants: to make us so busy with the cares of life that we cannot make the switch in our thoughts, actions, and efforts.

The Hebrew boys Shadrach, Meshach, and Abednego were faced with a great dilemma when they had to choose between life and death. Although their choice seemed like imminent death in this world, it was a choice of life in the spirit world. Paul said, *"We are confident, I say, and willing rather to be absent from the body, and to be present with the Lord"* (2 Corinthians 5:8).

We need to be deliberate in our response to negative situations and thoughts that come into our minds. We need to deliberately make the switch and begin to see through the mind of the Kingdom. When the cares of life overwhelms us, we must get our minds out of the system and pattern of this world and make the switch to the Kingdom, causing us to behave in the ways God would.

Once we start thinking like God, our minds will begin to work with the pattern of the Kingdom. In this Kingdom, we will begin to believe that we aren't defined by how much money we have, the house we live in, or what we wear. We aren't defined by what the doctors or lawyers say. We are defined by the fact that we are sons of God. When God calls us sons, it should not be taken lightly. We should think of ourselves as representing God. When Adam was in good standing with God, he was God's only connection to the earth. When we are the ones God has a connection with, and when we aren't in the right place, He searches for us. He wants to work through us. That's

Think Like God

why when Satan wants to destroy this connection, he goes after the mind. He knows that if he can keep us from thinking like God, he can keep us thinking like him. That means we will continue to worry, fear, hate, and doubt God.

Man's Way Versus God's Way

If we continue in this trend, we will never experience what God intended for us. But once we start thinking like God, we will see a change in our lives. We must pull down any thoughts that aren't God-like and switch our thought process if we are going to deal with situations victoriously.

Man's way of thinking says we should wait to receive before we can be grateful, but when we think like God we don't wait until things are actualized; we praise Him in advance, knowing that it shall come to pass. We can *"calleth those things which be not as though they were"* (Romans 4:17) because we know it's already done in the spirit world.

Man's way of thinking will cause us to fear the unknown, but a God-thinker will know they haven't received the spirit of fear but of power, love, and a sound mind (2 Timothy 1:7). We are in the hands of the One who holds our futures, and therefore we don't need to fear. He is the *"Alpha and Omega, the beginning and the end, the first and the last"* (Revelations 22:13). A God-thinker will know that the situation is already taken care of. The Omega has already seen the end of the situation and made a way.

Man's way of thinking will lead us to cower under the pressure of tribulations, but God's way of thinking will cause us to rejoice.

> *Beloved, think it not strange concerning the fiery trial which is to try you, as though some strange thing happened unto you: but rejoice, inasmuch as ye are partakers of Christ's sufferings; that, when his glory shall be revealed, ye may be glad also with exceeding joy.*
>
> —I Peter 4:12–13

When attacked, a God-thinker would say, *"[I have the] power to tread on serpents and scorpions, and over all the power of the enemy: and nothing shall by any means hurt [me]"* (Luke 10:19), or *"No weapon that is formed against thee shall prosper; and every tongue that shall rise against thee in judgment thou shalt condemn. This is the heritage of the servants of the Lord, and their righteousness is of me"* (Isaiah 54:17).

We can overcome anything the devil throws at us if we only acknowledge and accept the power we have and know that it all starts with a thought. As God's thoughts became the Word and His Word became life, we too can speak with authority if we have the mind of God. God's thoughts are full of power, action, and success. It accomplishes what it was sent to do, whether it was to create life or to bring back to life, whether it calmed the sea or created a storm, whether it turned water into wine or water into blood. Can you imagine what we can do if we would only believe? Jesus said, *"He that believeth on me, the works that I do shall he do also; and greater works than these shall he do"* (John 14:12).

I can speak life into a dead situation, I can bring hope to something that seems hopeless, if I will only allow the process to begin. Paul said *"I die daily"* (I Corinthians 15:31). Daily I release the things that control my thoughts. Daily I put away the doubt that creates distance between me and God. Daily I break down the things that block the thoughts of God.

After overcoming hindrances, discovering God in His Word, and understanding how God thinks, I conclude that we can move closer to what God wants us to be: God-thinkers! That is the ultimate result.

So let's go forward and think like God.